Trevor Pateman

The Best I Can Do

degree zero

First published 2016 by **degree zero** an imprint of Theyby Ltd
Unit 10, 91 Western Road
Brighton BN1 2NW, England

ISBN 978-0-9935879-0-0

246531

A CIP catalogue record for this book is available from
the British Library

Printed and Bound by CPI Group (UK) Ltd, Croydon CR0 4YY

The Best I Can Do

Contents

Inside back cover:
Illustration for Young Girl with a Fan?

Atheists, Agnostics & Abstainers

TEETOTALLERS (once called Total Abstainers) and Vegetarians are people who renounce something which they may well find attractive - in the case of alcoholics, too attractive. Some vegetarians are repelled by the thought of eating dead animal flesh. Others aren't - the novelist Jonathan Saffran Foer, for example, author of an extended defence of the vegetarian case, *Eating Animals* (2000). The smell of your barbecue wafting into his house triggers temptation not disgust. But for him the temptation is one to be resisted, on moral grounds.

I sometimes think of myself as abstaining from religion, both from practice and belief. Some religious things I find repulsive but not all of them. There seem to be attractive aspects to all religions, though I only have experience of one. But when you start to put things in the balance, for me the scales always tip one way.

Start with religious practices. I won't attend an infant christening. I think it's morally wrong - mildly abusive - to take your new born child and sign them straight up for something which ought to be a matter for considered choice. When I was baptised into the Church of England in 1947 my godparents (I remember their names but nothing more) were handed little cards to instruct them in their Duties and my parents got a copy which I inherited. It is headed *Take this child and nurse it for Me* [capital M in the original] and instructs Mr and Mrs Mardell:

1. *To pray regularly for my Godchild.*
2. *To ask myself frequently: Does my Godchild know, or is he being taught the promises which he made by me* [that is to say, through the godparent] *at his Baptism, namely: (a) to renounce the devil and all his works, the vain pomp and glory of the world, with all covetous desires of the same, and the carnal desires of the flesh ... ?*

Yes, that and more is what I am supposed to have promised as a mewling babe in arms with these godparents I don't know from Adam taking power of attorney because of my own inability to say the words "I promise". There is an appropriate response to this preposterous claim that I made any promises at all, shortly after my birth, and it's only two words long. I don't know whether my godparents prayed for me - I suspect not - but looking at the Archbishop of Canterbury it's quite clear that his godparents did not pray very hard when it came to the vain pomp and glory bit. That's cheap, I know, but like many *ad hominem* arguments, it's true.

I have always been willing to attend a church funeral service and, recently, I attended a church wedding. I wouldn't want either for myself but if other adults want such things, I suppose I should show some ecumenical spirit, always remembering that it actually means some joining in. I offer up a compromise to the Church of England: I sing the hymns but I stay silent, eyes open, during the prayers.

I wouldn't attend the genital mutilation of an infant or a

child or a party to celebrate a mutilation. In fact, I think circumcisions - of both boys and girls - should be illegal. Children deserve state protection from such assaults on their bodies. I am even surprised when parents want to pierce their infant children's ears. But since the result is reversible, I am not appalled by it in the way that a circumcision appals me. I just think that babies and children are such delightful creatures that I can't see why you would want to do anything other than take pleasure in them the way they are and hope, sometimes anxiously, that their bodies will sustain them into adult life. Children aren't toys and their bodies aren't yours.

When parents have to decide for their young child whether to allow necessary or recommended medical surgery, then I think they have a terrible decision to make. However hard you try to explain, a young child will not fully understand. You will witness their pain, which may not be easy to assuage, and you will witness and feel their loss of trust - in you and in the world. I can't think of any good "religious" reasons for wanting those things to happen to your child when there is no justification of medical necessity.

What about beliefs? My childhood experiences - I am talking about my mother - were of religious beliefs which were essentially punitive and which fed and watered eventually unbearable levels of guilt, anxiety, despair, melancholy. My mother's default state was to feel herself damned. These were the kinds of belief into which it would have been easy to fall myself and from which I had - eventually - to make an effort to abstain. But I also felt anger at the punitive religious culture, Victorian and Edwardian (my mother was born in 1907 and her mother in 1867), which burdened my mother for her whole life. The priests in black gowns who made it their business to induce such feelings in the vulnerable were to me loathsome creatures. They should be ostracised. The feelings have lasted a life time.

When Tony Blair and Gordon Brown and finally David Cameron sucked up to Pope Benedict sufficiently for him to deign to visit Scotland and England and when all the political class sucked up to him at Westminster - just one elected MP signing a letter of protest against the visit - I felt anger and contempt. Who was this man? A reactionary professor who had dedicated his life to making things uncomfortable for those in his church who tried to make it more humane. A man whose whole life had been dedicated to the cause of institutional self-preservation. It's not as if he had oil wells or produced everything we consume; our obsequiousness was entirely voluntary

Worse, we rolled out the red carpet at the very moment when the government of the Republic of Ireland was trying to hold to account its Roman Catholic Church and the Vatican hierarchy which had stood behind it while it abused its way for decades through many thousands of children entrusted to its care. There was real fury in Ireland and Pope Benedict could not have set foot there. We fawned to him, but Ireland withdrew its Ambassador to the Vatican and expelled the Papal Nuncio in Dublin. Even here, outside the political class, there was a flicker of understanding – but from the strangest quarter: HSBC – the Hong Kong and Shanghai Banking Corporation, no less - forcibly closed the London bank account of the Pope's Nuncio, his Ambassador to London, concluding that it belonged with a bunch of Third World dictator accounts as a probable vehicle for money laundering. But our politicians and the *Opus Dei* desk at the BBC only had headlines for Benedict. You could see the election of Pope Francis as a rebuke to our political class. He may change the Roman Catholic Church but, unfortunately, he won't change our politicians.

Religious organisations have caused and continue to cause immense harm in the world. The history of Catholicism is a history of callousness and inhumanity, continuing to this day. Worse, I only single it out because I know so little of the history of other religions and religious organisations. But I know enough to acknowledge that the clerical class in modern Saudi Arabia obviously does a good job convincing the rest of the world that religion and humanity are opposed to each other.

And so, by and large, one must abstain. Religion is unclean, contaminated perhaps not at source but certainly by history. I sometimes think of what I practice as "Moral Unbelief" - it doesn't feel *right* to believe and, if possible, one should *avoid* religious belief and religious practices.

*

Theological discussions normally focus on questions such as Does God Exist? - which is called an ontological question – or on questions such as How Do We Know God Exists? – an epistemological question. There are lots of books on both topics, written over millennia, and currently sustaining the activities of publicly-funded university departments of theology. But I don't find these questions very interesting. I have read some of the books - John Hicks's long, scholarly and inconclusive *Evil and The God of Love* (1966), for example. But I am happy to leave the writing of them to the academics, minus the public funding.

If you *feel* that God exists, that seems to me an intelligible feeling and one not to be sneered at. But, Be Careful! There is a slippery slope from intelligible feelings to signing up to religious organisations with terrible histories of hatred of children, women and anyone who doesn't agree with them. In a 2012 book which starts in an I'm-a-regular-sort-of-guy way and then turns into a Biblical fundamentalist tract - *Unapologetic, why, despite everything, Christianity can still make surprising emotional sense* - Francis Spufford recognises the slippery slope and slides down with glee: it's the Leap of Faith, he cries, as he renounces the tab of E. (page 66 of his book) for the dubious ecstasy of the Church of England. The author clearly has critical faculties but simply decides to ditch them in favour of happy-clappy fun on Sunday mornings. That's not good enough.

Working to advance the secularisation of society is much more important than arguing the toss about God. The high clergy fulminate against "aggressive secularists" – notably helped on this by the BBC when, for example, it regularly gave Cardinal Keith O'Brien top news coverage for his aggressive anti-secularist sermons - because secularism threatens the worldly power (and the bishops' palaces) of the churches. But the same clergy are often happy to cosy up to the atheists. They think that Richard Dawkins is really one of them. He probably is since there are probably atheists among the bishops.

In Italy, back in 1929, the Roman Catholic Church secured from Mussolini its independence from Italian legal jurisdiction. The "city state" created by the Lateran treaty was allowed to go its own (criminal) way and became Italy's other Mafia. If you want to really upset the Vatican forget about abortion and contraception - just propose that Italy should repudiate the Lateran Treaty, send in the tanks and re-incorporate the Vatican into its own territory. Much more effective than debating *Does God Exist?*

The prolonged conflicts in the Middle East have at least something to do with the collision between secularisers (who may well be theists rather than atheists) and reactionary clergies (Shia, Sunni – they can unite on this) determined to hold on to worldly power and still having far too much success.

Here in England, most adults nowadays don't go near religion from one year to the next. That's sound and healthy. But they tolerate large doses of it administered to their children on government order. For some reason, and unusually for adults, British politicians Do God all the time. I think it's the expenses fiddling. They use such power as they still retain to insist that children Do God too.

If a good God did exist, he would not wish us to believe in him anymore. His name has been invoked to justify far too many crimes. We should withdraw our complicity and, especially, our money. Abstention in this case is a principled and effective position.

Bus Passes & Benefits

I've never claimed my Free Bus Pass. I would be ashamed to wave it while paying passengers watch. Imagine that it was Coloreds who paid and Whites who didn't .Where I live, looking at workers boarding the bus and paying their fares on the way to low-paid jobs, that's not far from the reality. Nor is it far from the reality that poor people pay and better-off Over Sixties don't. Yet the Over Sixties, quite solidly and sometimes fiercely, now seem to believe that they have a Human Right to bus travel paid for by others – even though Bus Passes are a very recent invention. How did this come about? The fault lies with our political parties, always looking for cheap ways to gain the favour of those most likely to vote. Any party now proposing to withdraw the passes would face a backlash of unreasoned wrath. My Benefits, right or wrong!

Bus Passes are not Pensioner Passes. You qualify by virtue of reaching your 60th birthday, well below the ages at which most people qualify for state pensions. At sixty, many people are still working, their children are gone and they have paid off mortgages. They are better off than at any time before. Many of those waving Bus Passes – of course, not all – are better dressed than they have ever been. They can afford to be. Eventually, they will become old and even frail. It's always stressful to watch a frail elderly person board a bus, struggling with shopping bags and sticks. They don't need a Bus Pass any more. They need a once-a-week Taxi Pass.

Or, rather, they need adequate pensions. Free bus passes are not only electoral bribes; they are also one of the cosmetic means by which feckless governments have sought to disguise the inadequacy of State Pension provision in the UK. In relation to former earnings, that pension is much lower than the European average: about one third against an average of a half across twenty-seven other European nations. Our governments have been too fearful to force people to pay enough into retirement income schemes to fund adequate pensions and reluctant - until absolutely forced by a huge rise in life expectancy- to raise the pensionable age. Until very recently in the UK, the State Pension age for women was set at sixty. Men at sixty-five.

No one challenged that extraordinary bit of entrenched sex discrimination. It had its origins in discriminatory thinking: women filled up the workforce during two world wars and thus qualified for pensions. But allowing them to take their pensions at sixty was also meant to ease them out of the workforce, leaving more room for men who had fought. Over time, the discrimination transformed from discrimination against women to discrimination in their favour. But for decades no one challenged it.

Self-respect is very much connected to the ability to make your own choices. Older people generally benefit from walking or even cycling but politicians want you to take the bus. The bus companies are happy enough; they get paid. The Bus Pass is a clunking decision by politicians to make choices for you: Here, my good woman, take this

Pass and use that bus over there! And show some gratitude! In a better world, older people would dispose of enough income to make their own choices and thus maintain an important aspect of personal dignity. It would be acceptable to withdraw the Bus Passes and add to the State Pension the equivalent of the money saved. All that you lose is the self-satisfied smile of the politician who wants you to doff your cap and thank him (Gordon Brown, Ken Livingstone).

*

The Bus Pass is a symptom of a deeper problem which resides at the core of the British Treasury and the way it relates to British governments. The Treasury hates two things above all: ring fenced money and entitlements. It is committed to the ideas that all revenues should go into a single big undifferentiated Pot under its own control and that all outgoings, whether to government departments or citizens, are a matter of discretion.

That is, of course, an understandable way for a Treasury to think. It gives you the maximum of flexibility in what is often – thanks to politicians – a struggle to make the books balance. But it is also completely symbiotic with the interest of party politicians. They too want maximum discretion. Let me give one example.

British prime ministers now normally want to pick at least one war to fight during their time in office. These wars of choice can be vote-winners. They allow the prime minister to walk tall. Mr Cameron was deeply disappointed in 2013 when he was not able to get his war in Syria, supporting Syrian *jihadis*. He had better luck in 2015 when

Parliament agreed to his new plan to attack *jihadis* in Syria. It put him up there with the Big Boys.

But equally a government going to war does not want voters to think about the financial costs. The last thing it wants is being forced to impose a War Tax. That would make voters think twice about their gung-ho enthusiasms for bombing far away countries. Fortunately, the Treasury pot is usually big enough to absorb the costs of a small war, one which sticks to the cheap route to failure, that of bombing civilians. Money can be shifted between notional budgets and, if not, borrowing can be discreetly increased. But when monies are ring-fenced and there are entitlements, it becomes more difficult. As a result of this way of thinking, both Treasury and politicians are committed to the ideas (though they would never admit it) that *All Benefits are Voluntary Hand Outs* and *No Benefits are Entitlements.* In other words, citizens have no rights.

The obvious way to create entitlement to benefits is through insurance schemes. People pay into the scheme and, at the same time, they are informed of their entitlements under the scheme. That is what Britain's National Insurance system was once supposed to be about. But now it isn't. No one pays in anywhere near enough to accumulate entitlement to the benefits they can claim. Nowadays, it is merely a concession to the idea that there can be benefits to which you are entitled because you have insured for them. If the Treasury had its way, even that concession would be abolished. The Treasury loathes the idea of insurance. It gets in the way of tax and spend.

The Treasury has almost a winning hand in one simple fact about our psychology. We hate it when we see money removed from our pay packet before we even get it: Pay as You Earn taxes, National Insurance. If National Insurance was for realistic sums of money we would hate it even more. But when it comes to paying 20% Value Added Tax on virtually everything we buy – well, we don't even notice it (often we don't see it separately itemised). This is the Treasury's winning hand – taxes we don't notice. Not only that, such invisible taxes are not linked to any specific government expenditures. The Treasury gets just the kind of money it wants, money it can use as it (or its political masters) please. In addition, VAT quietly and effectively reverses the progressive character of Income Tax and produces the desired overall result that the poor pay a higher percentage of their income in tax than the rich.

The symbiotic Treasury - Politician commitment to avoiding entitlements and favouring handouts immediately opens the door to the parlour game known as *Benefits Scrounging,* in which the winners are those who work out every handout for which they can make themselves eligible and promptly claim them all. Those who celebrate their 60th birthday by claiming their Free Bus Pass are benefits scroungers. They have no entitlement to the pass, they have done nothing to deserve it, they often don't need it – but it's there, a handout, yours for the asking.

*

We have an increasingly shaky idea of what it means to be a citizen. The benefits culture, created by politicians and sustained until very recently by an all-party consensus, has been disempowering. It encourages childishness at election times as voters shop around looking for the party which offers three for the price of two. No more than that. No expectation that you think about the future, about your children and grandchildren; certainly no expectation that you think about right and wrong, justice and fairness.

An obvious route towards re-building ideas of citizenship involves, among much else, dismantling the Handouts culture and re-instating the idea of a contributory system: you pay in for health care, unemployment benefit, and pensions. That must be the expectation for nearly everyone, with a non-contributory but generous social safety net principally for those who are born disabled or become so. It also involves challenging the Treasury - Politician collusion. There is no reason why money should not be ring-fenced, why taxes on X should not go towards paying for Y and only for Y. If politicians want a war, then they must use a War Tax to pay for it. If voters want a war, then they should be obliged to put their money where their flags wave.

Probably the only interesting alternative to this approach is the idea of a universal Citizen Entitlement to a flat monthly income about big enough to live on. Everyone would get it, regardless of income or age. For those in work, for example, it would simply lower their tax bill. For those not earning, for whatever reason, it would be a handout but without the disfiguring features of the electoral bribes currently on offer to selected groups, most obviously and repeatedly in the UK, the voting over 60s.

The idea has the merit of threatening the destruction of a thousand benefits bureaucracies, most of which end up in the newspapers for incompetence of one kind or another. So it is a sleek proposal. It has the de-merits that it hands money to people who don't need it and, in practice, will still have to include small print provisions for special cases like those of people whose disabilities oblige them to make use of expensive equipment or carers. From where I am coming from, universal citizen entitlement has the demerit that it puts all citizens in the position of state dependents. I have yet to read an argument that persuades me that is not the case.

Crimes & Punishments

MOST crimes are inconsequential: the perpetrator does not gain very much and the victim does not lose very much.

Nearly every victim of crime has what I call a *Crime Excess*, rather like the Excess on a Driving or House Insurance policy which sets the level below which you will deal with the matter yourself. (I always pick the highest figure offered). The Crime Excess sets the level below which you will not report the matter to the police.

Some people will go to the police if they think they have suffered what I will informally quantify as £50 worth of harm; others will only go if the harm exceeds £1000. But most people will also take into account the costs of reporting a crime. Make the police less accessible - fewer police, fewer police stations, longer queues - and the average harm level at which people will go to the police will rise. So reported crime will fall. It's cause and effect: less policing causes less (reported) crime. Some people will think that some things are so trivial that they should not *bother* an overworked police with them. Others will think about the hassle, the waits in line, the low probability of the police doing anything, the even lower probability of anything coming to court … and they will quite reasonably decide it's not *worth* going to the police.

Years ago now, I was leaving my office in the city of

Brighton & Hove. As I turned around from locking the door I noticed three or four teenage boys on the other side of the road. For some reason they started cat-calling me. I found that odd: I wasn't wearing my funny hat (I sometimes wear funny hats) and I wasn't behaving oddly. I was clearly someone leaving work. Maybe they were a bit drunk. Daytime drunkenness is not unknown in the city. So I simply began my walk home. The boys stayed on the other side of the road and continued to jeer. Then something whizzed across the road and an egg struck the pavement in front of me. I looked across the road and the boys ran away. I walked home thinking, What was that all about? Mistaken identity?

In those circumstances, someone with a mental £50 Crime Excess would have phoned the police station and reported the incident. Maybe the police would have been interested if it added to a pattern of reports. Maybe they would have asked for a statement; maybe not. But I have a £1000 Crime Excess in my head. I preferred to go home, eat my dinner, and read my book. I had no desire to spend time on the phone to the police, reporting a very small incident. In any case, I could not have given any useful description of the boys. Had the incident been repeated, then I would no doubt have begun to approach my £1000 Crime Excess and maybe on a third occasion I would have reached it. But the boys never re-appeared and as far as crime statistics are concerned, nothing ever happened. That seems to me a state of affairs which ought to be satisfactory to everyone except the professional student of crime.

As for perpetrators of crime, it often does more harm than good for anyone to be caught and prosecuted, if only because of the waste of time involved and the enormous cost to the public purse. For example, I would rather that teenage shoplifters didn't get caught – or, at least, didn't get dealt with by the police and the courts. Teenagers will soon grow out of it; only if they don't is some other response to the crime necessary. A court appearance is almost certainly going to be overkill.

So we should have laws on the statute books which citizens will always think twice about invoking and the police about enforcing. It makes for a more civilised society if most citizens don't end up with criminal records.

In some countries, the sense of this attitude is recognised in statutes of limitations: if you aren't caught and tried within a period of time - variable according to the gravity of the offence - then the slate is wiped clean and you can no longer be investigated or prosecuted. You may even choose to admit to the offence at some future date, if it helps you to confess or helps someone else to know who did it.

The trouble with this approach is that it is open to abuse, as anyone who followed the spectacle of Silvio Berlusconi's financial and sexual affairs can immediately point out. If you are wealthy, you can employ fancy lawyers to spin out cases until they have to be dropped just because they have reached their expiry date. Law-abiding citizens are then left with the sense that someone who ought to be in prison isn't and only because of his wealth. This is why other countries don't have statutes of limitations, leaving it to the discretion of the police when to drop a case or decline to open one which just seems very old and best forgotten. That discretion can also be abused, of course. Ordinary citizens guilty of more modest crimes may be less lucky than Lord Lucan.

In England, we do effectively have a statute of limitations in relation to drug offences. This is what enables our politicians to confess to "youthful experiments" confident that a police constable will not arrive at their door to take down a confession of possession. But it does not stop those same politicians from keeping drug laws on the statute books to be thrown at the youth of today. This simply confirms the rest of us in our belief that to succeed as a politician you have to be good at double standards.

An expiry date (One year? One month?) on the criminal offence would be one way of moving away from the fear of sensible discussion of drugs law. I can't see that it would give rise to much by way of Berlusconi-style abuse. The same is true of most sexual offences, where an expiry date (Ten years? Five years?) would stop the bizarre British practice of forcing jurors to decide who is telling the truth about what did or did not happen in the office cupboard one afternoon thirty or even forty years ago. In the absence of other evidence, the risk of miscarriage of justice is too great, for both parties, even if one ignores the dubious motivations of the police in cases where celebrities are involved. Baffled juries set impossible tasks will free the guilty and send the innocent to jail. Worse, it is unclear that criminal proceedings at such distances are things which victims generally want. Police and prosecutors sometimes pursue old cases which victims would like to abandon. In such cases, outsiders may want the show trial more than those who will inevitably be on show in the prosecution witness box. The victim can end up victim again, as part of a spectacle. [See Endnote]

*

Laws should be enforced in moderation. One main reason we need to talk about America is that its approach to law enforcement has ended up criminalising a significant part of the population, notably the very large proportion of young black males who end up with prison records. It is dysfunctional at so many levels that we should work very hard to avoid assisting it, not least by declining to throw UK citizens to American justice via one-sided extradition agreements. America has 5% of the world's population and 25% of the prison population, with an incarceration rate of 698 persons per 100 000 population making it the world's Number Two jail way ahead of Cuba (510), Russia (446) and tin pot dictatorship Belarus (306). Some of those prisoners are kept in terrifying conditions. We should not feed a sadistic system. Nor should we feed our own bloated prison system, which currently houses 148 people per 100 000, comfortably ahead of France (100) and Germany (76) and, of course, way ahead of the usual suspects for doing everything better than we do, the Scandinavian countries.

Nearly everyone deserves a second chance before they are sent to prison. There are good, self-interested reasons for thinking like that. In general, there are benefits from co-operation which exceed the benefits from conflict. Most games are not zero-sum games in which my gain is your loss and vice versa. So when someone who you relied on to co-operate in a potentially positive sum game fails to do so, the rational response is to give them another chance - and, if possible, to signal that this is what you are doing. But if they fail to co-operate a second time, then you go into conflict mode and strike back hard. In other words, *A Tit for Two Tats*.

Many of the crimes committed during urban rioting, like those London and Paris periodically experience, are opportunistic. Many of those caught are the most naive - the people who did not cover their faces or who did not know how to run fast when confronted. Many of them will have no previous criminal record. They are the wrong people on which to exercise Tit for Tat. The heavy sentences should be imposed on those who have done it - or something similar - before. If you Make An Example of first-time amateurs you do something similar to that which police forces do when they go after low-hanging fruit – crimes and criminals easy to pick off – at the same time quietly ignoring scary or difficult big time crime.

It is foolish to criminalise large numbers of people who you actually *need* not to be criminals, but to become hard-working and law-abiding citizens. The only rational policy is to give them a second chance. To do otherwise is simply to begin the process by which an offender becomes a repeat offender and society becomes a zero-sum game.

*

Thefts not involving violence should be punished by a fine. Whoever seeks to enrich himself at the expense of others should be deprived of his own. But, since this is ordinarily the crime only of poverty and desperation, the crime of that unhappy portion of mankind to whom the right of property...has left but a bare existence ...the most suitable punishment will be that kind of servitude which alone can be called just - the temporary subjection of the labours and person of the criminal to the community, as repayment ...

Cesare Beccaria, On Crimes and Punishments
(1764; Paolucci's translation)

*

If you take a long view, then certainly as far as property and theft is concerned the right way of proceeding becomes decidedly unclear and positively murky the longer the view into history becomes.

There are still children and grandchildren of Holocaust victims successfully claiming back goods (usually art works) stolen by the Nazis. The works have often ended up in some German museum or Swiss bank vault. Such restitution is justice done and seen to be done; it is frequently reported. But such cases may obscure the fact that, if only we had better documentation, we would soon discover that *most claims to ownership of significant assets are invalid*. At some point, the chain of legitimate exchange and inheritance has been broken by force or fraud.

Of course, most things which are stolen - whether by invading armies or criminal gangs or rapacious capitalists - have only a short shelf-life. When in the past hungry soldiers stole a peasant's crops, they did so to eat them. The peasant may later have been able to claim compensation. But I doubt that one in ten thousand peasants was ever compensated. In some cases, they would have been killed for the impertinence of asking.

A few things have a long shelf-life - land, houses, jewels, art works, books and papers. My hypothesis is that, around the world, the title to most such things is bad. At some point, the line of succession and exchange was broken by force or fraud - the force of a common thief, an invading army, a usurper king, a vicious kleptocrat; the fraud of a contract with duplicitous small print. That is our inheritance. But only in a few cases will it be possible to document that the present title is bad and in still fewer will it be possible to say who has a better title, except generically. Native

Americans and Aborigines as groups have a better claim to own the land of America and Australia than those individuals whose ownership is today upheld by the United States or the Commonwealth of Australia. But since the native populations have been pushed to the point of extinction – Sunday afternoon aborigine hunts in a few parts of Australia continued into the 1930s – there are very few people who seriously believe they should get it all back, despite the terrible crimes which have been committed on the way to today's status quo.

In contrast, there are still plenty of Palestinians who can document individually what they have lost. And quite a few Armenians and Armenian institutions - which is one reason why Turkey is unwilling to concede the Armenian Genocide claim. (As an aside, I sometimes imagine that if Turkey handed to Armenian jurisdiction the national symbol of that country, Mount Ararat, then reciprocally Armenia would drop all other claims against Turkey. It would be an imaginative move on both sides and is therefore unlikely to happen). In the Armenian case, as in the case of the Holocaust, there are also significant claims against third parties – for example, foreign banks which simply held onto a great deal of money in the accounts of Armenians who vanished in World War One and foreign insurance companies which did not pay out on Life policies. None of them made any efforts to track down rightful owners or beneficiaries. But suppose we in turn asked how the Armenians came by their property and their wealth and went back farther into history? I think it would become murky again.

I don't think anyone living in England knows that they are descendants of natives who lost everything in the Norman Conquest or even in later forcible redistributions.

In principle, the Roman Catholic Church could probably document fairly exactly what it lost in Henry VIIIs dissolution of the monasteries and could put together a claim for restitution or compensation, but I doubt anyone would take it seriously. It was all too long ago and the Roman Catholic Church is without moral authority anyway. Most importantly, however, the dissolution of the monasteries was enacted through state legislation and therefore counts as nothing worse than "nationalisation without compensation".

Time does make a difference. Hang on to stolen property for long enough and eventually everyone concedes that it is yours. The Royal Borough of Kensington and Chelsea, to take a notorious example, is now owned to some unknown but probably considerable extent by foreigners who have taken bribes, stolen state funds, laundered the proceeds of crime. Some have probably hired killers along the way. A whole London-based industry of facilitators exists to support this conversion of black money to sash windows. Right now, it would not be unreasonable for the British state to nationalise without compensation foreign-owned London property, rather as it confiscates the assets of its own regular criminals. But in due course, as Kensington and Chelsea passes to the children and grandchildren of the original crooks, confiscation will come to seem unreasonable. After all, what would happen to our own aristocracy if we probed too deeply into its past? Plantations, slave-trading, raiding parties, war loot, land theft, enclosure acts …. It is this line of thinking which has motivated British governments to spin out the legal cases brought against them by the expelled inhabitants of the British Indian Ocean Territory (Diego Garcia / Chagos Islands) clearly reckoning that as the original inhabitants die off – they were expelled nearly fifty years ago now – the case will go away. And it probably will.

In many ways, the problem history poses is like that which personal relationships pose, How do we punctuate events? He says "You started it" and she says "No, You started it" and a patient counsellor works backwards and finds that the issue of who started it is lost in the mists of time. So it is in history, often but not always. Crimes and punishments are things about which, on the long view, there is often not much basis for anyone to get on a high horse. By and large, our criminal justice systems should focus their energies on recent and serious crimes against the person. It is in those cases that societies should show more determination to protect their citizens, especially children and the vulnerable. That is supposed to be one of the fundamental things that states are for. It is the crimes of today – especially the murders, rapes, assaults and intimidation - that matter most, not the crimes of the past. And most crimes should become Past their Punishable Date very quickly.

*

Endnote:

An example from another domain – the Holocaust - where prosecutions are still being pursued seventy years after the event. In 1963 – not even twenty years after the event - Simon Wiesenthal, the famous "Nazi Hunter", tracked down the SS Officer, Karl Silberbauer, who in 1944 arrested Anne Frank and others living in the Secret Annex in Amsterdam. Silberbauer had subsequently become a police officer in Vienna. He was suspended pending investigation and Anne's father, Otto Frank, reluctantly attended the disciplinary hearing. He had lost his wife and daughters to the Nazis. But he felt that the (unknown) person who denounced the Franks to the Nazis bore greatest responsibility for what happened to his family and testified neutrally that Silberbauer had only done his duty and had behaved correctly. Otto Frank also said that the only thing he asked for was not to have to see Silberbauer again. Silberbauer was re-instated as a police officer. As I read it, Otto Frank in effect thwarted any attempt Wiesenthal might have wanted (and probably did want) to make to bring Silberbauer before a court at which Otto Frank would have been a star witness. The publicity around the discovery of Silberbauer was important because there were Holocaust deniers who were saying that Anne Frank never existed whereas Silberbauer confirmed his role in arresting her and volunteered details he had remembered. He did not seem repentant but that was not what Otto Frank was looking for anyway. He was trying to get on with his life and make something of it, which he did by helping to ensure that the life and work of his daughter Anne was properly recognised. The vigilantes of Justice can't really cope with the idea that people have different ways of coming to terms with trauma and grief and that in some cases they will feel that courts of law will be a hindrance, not a help.

Death Rituals

WHEN someone you have responsibility for dies, there are things you have to do, many of them highly conventionalised so that you don't have to think too much: notifications, funerals, in some cases burials and gravestones, clearing a house and executing a will. I suspect we could do it better than we do if we weren't so afraid that we might disturb the spirit of the dead person or if we weren't forced to do it all in the middle of grief.

Funerals are organised by the living who also have to experience them. It is better that the dead do not interfere. Their taste in music is usually dire. It's possible to dispose of a body without a funeral: you send it to the crematorium and they burn it. No one has to take a day off work. It seems a bit harsh, though there was a time when I would have chosen it for myself: the teenage time when *The Mayor of Casterbridge* allowed me to indulge maudlin grief to the full. Most likely, my children will have to decide whether to give me a funeral and, if so, of what kind. I trust they will have my body cremated and spare me any religious officiation. Otherwise, it's up to them how they use the time they will be allocated. I don't envy them and, if they go with cremation and No Vicar, I promise to spare them my musical tastes.

Nowadays, parents often live to an age when their

children have resolved the difficulties parents have created for them and where they can feel that the parents have had their life and it is right that they should die. This is helpful; it is hard when a child, even a thirty- or forty- year old child, is cut off from a parent before some resolution of old disputes and difficulties has been achieved. But some kind of resolution is never the end of the story. When you talk to people who have lost a parent or a partner, even one very old and sick, it is clear that the expectation of someone's death is always not quite real. Death is not meant to happen this week, when you are not quite ready. A funeral is one of the ways we deal with the fact of not having been quite ready for a death.

*

A grave in a cemetery can be a way of postponing the business of dealing with a death. I have never been back to the crematoria where the bodies of my parents were burnt. The truth is, I think it best that ashes are scattered to the wind. In Paris, I once did the tourist visit to Père Lachaise and was moved by the narrative on the tomb of Héloise and Abelard, re-united in death, but merely curious in relation to Jim Morrison and all the rest. Stuck for something to do when on business trips, I have sometimes strolled a local cemetery, highly visible in Catholic countries. But they are awful places, combining crude assertion of social rank and inevitable neglect - and creepy when there are photographs of the dead. In Vienna, I went down into the vaults where the emperors are boxed up. The ritual surrounding this, in which the pall bearers have to knock for admittance, strikes me as similar in intent to the ritual demanded by Wahabbi

Islam - that rulers be buried in unmarked graves, a much better idea than our own devotion to monumental masons. But in Jerusalem, back in 1995, I made a very deliberate effort to visit the grave of Oskar Schindler. And I was prepared with a tiny bit of Sussex flint to place on the grave and I took photographs. I don't understand this aberration in my normal attitudes towards graves.

*

My mother's ambition was to bequeath £1000 to her only son. When she died in 1978, aged 71, her Post Office Savings Bank account wasn't quite in four figures though she had been saving for a long time from money I gave her each month. It was a strange side-effect of grief that I tried very hard, irrationally hard, to get as much as I could for her bits of furniture and knick-knacks and eventually persuaded myself that she had achieved her ambition. I needed to feel that she had achieved something, anything.

It is common for those who inherit to transmute grief into obsession with the inheritance, and sometimes it all gets mixed up with unresolved sibling rivalries and with ordinary greed. I was once told the story of four siblings who on the death of their mother inherited a gold chain necklace and really nothing else. So they cut it in four. Maybe it was to have a keepsake; but as it was told to me, it was to have gold. It's likely that I remember that story because my own sneaking sympathies are with the Gypsies of the past. I think they got it nearly right. Everything should go up in smoke. It will prevent a great deal of unseemly behaviour.

However, in order that my pyromaniac tendencies shan't alarm my own children, they have been given most of their inheritance already. I no longer own The House which is the core of modern British inheritances and which is the focus of so much anxiety and emotion that it is credited with having obliged British Prime Minister Gordon Brown to abandon the snap election he had hoped to call in 2007. The Tories, his political opponents, fearing defeat if an election was called, sabotaged the whole plan with just one promise: *We will raise the Inheritance Tax Threshold to £1 million* - something which Brown had recently ruled against. Now it's on the statute books, as unchallengeable as Bus Passes.

Early Learning

HUMAN babies are born incapable of surviving without assistance and that assistance is required for a few years. This helplessness may encourage the view that babies are also mindless, their empty minds needing filling just like their empty stomachs. I think that is wrong. Babies are born with very powerful minds which are able to make fairly rapid sense of the world around them and begin to act upon it.

They are capable of this despite the fact that a great deal of what they experience has a random and almost unstructured character. If adults had to cope with such randomness, they would give up and often do. But powerful baby minds enable babies to go beyond the information given and generate structures or theories within which they can understand and respond to the world in which they find themselves.

Two things are especially important in this "early learning". Some things are simply disregarded to await later attention or, as some would say, for a later stage. It takes a while before babies get interested in trying to speak and though you can advance their interest a bit, you can't advance it much. Adults just have to wait for it to start happening. Try too early and it will all be water off a duck's back. If you want your child to be a speaking prodigy, forget it. No baby is interested and if, extraordinarily, your baby is – well, you have just happen to have brought into the world one of those very, very rare things, a true speaking prodigy. No credit to you, though. Your child is simply one of Nature's kinder freaks.

All children, prodigies or not, develop a language before they know what they are doing. It just happens and the mental course it takes is partly ring-fenced against (premature) attempts at teaching and training. As far as a very young child is concerned, the plural of *sheep* is *sheeps* and for a long time if you try to correct that you will do so in vain. Language *grows* in the child and the mental resources which make that possible also determine that every language grown is at the same time broadly similar to others in local use - enough so that the child can be understood - but also at least a little different, so that adults can feel that there are things to be corrected. (Such correction is not offered in the interest of understanding; you can only correct that which you have already perfectly well understood).

The second thing is this. Babies are a bit like self-programming computers: give them a bit of stimulus, a bit of information and they generate a program to make sense of it and future encounters of the same kind. But their programs are very, very unlikely to be the same as those of surrounding adults. Babies have minds of their own and they aren't like yours. Their programs work differently. That is why their early drawings don't look like the ones you make and show them, probably assuming that they will admire and copy you. They don't. They just carry on until some change in their program is triggered. Such changes are often in what you will regard as the right direction but sometimes not.

When babies and toddlers seem to go backwards it is very, very unlikely that they have become lazy or rebellious, suffer from inadequate Discipline with a capital D or are being sent to the wrong nursery. No, what is much more likely happening is that they have gone back to the drawing board – though they don't think of it like that; it is all below the level of conscious awareness. They have encountered some difficulty operating a current program and they are starting over again. They are going backwards in order the better to leap forward. It happens in language development, in the development of arithmetical abilities, in drawing and probably even in fastening their shoes. All that parents have to do is be patient, not interfere (I'll compromise: not interfere too much) and just go on loving their child. It will all sort itself out and probably next week.

It might encourage parental patience if it was more widely realised that even if the child could pay attention to advice and correction and wasn't programmed simply to disregard such well-meaning stuff, the minds of adults are just not up to the full magnitude of the task of guiding the child. Adults simply cannot formulate, articulate and hold in their heads the rules of the systems they are trying to develop in the child and protect from error and change. On some fronts maybe they are quite good, like counting from one to ten without mistake. But parents can't do grammar very well and what we call "prescriptive grammar" is always a disaster zone, understood neither by those to whom it is prescribed or those who prescribe it. Finally, there are some fronts, such as the sound system of their language, where they are hopeless. The way words are pronounced, the intonation pattern of utterances - these are things which change all the time and generally below the threshold of awareness. Even when noticed, changes are impossible to characterise and manage as they are happening. Time passes, children find their way into roughly the right ball park quite effortlessly and - as far as intonation is concerned - what they develop lasts a life time. But their own children will in turn find their way into a slightly shifted ball park, and so it goes on. Adults don't really get a look in.

*

For much of my academic career, I was reading work on early child development though it was not a subject I taught. I read psychoanalytically focussed work (Freud, John Bowlby, Melanie Klein, Donald Winnicott) which makes security and feeling loved the basis of development in the child. I read the developmental studies pioneered by Piaget and followed through by Jerome Bruner, Howard Gardiner and many others and which give us the idea of *stages* of development. I specialised in Chomsky and Chomskyan approaches to language development which provide the ideas of *triggering* and *growth* in contrast to *teaching* and *learning*. Then there was stuff by pedagogues, old and new: A S Neill of Summerhill School and Seymour Papert of child-controlled robots fame. Even Rousseau got read because he has lots to say in *Émile* about children and their education. Last but not least, I had two children.

The paragraphs which opened this essay summarise what I have come to believe. How do I know it's the right way of looking at things, the right way of looking at infants? Well, you could say, I don't and partly because not every-thing I am trying to say is a testable scientific claim. Much of it is no more than a way of looking at things – or, rather, a way of looking at babies and toddlers. It starts from the sense that they are very unlike you and me (I can be pretty sure that there are no babies and toddlers among that "you") and a belief that their difference should be *accepted* even if that, as it sometimes does, involves a great deal of self-restraint (which is not even reciprocated!). The belief that they should be accepted pretty much as they are is not a scientific position; it's a moral belief. The German critic Walter Benjamin expressed something very close to what I feel when he wrote that "Children are Representatives of Paradise" – which sounds to me like a very good reason for paying attention to them just as we find them.

They are different but very definitely not less deserving of respect. When I talk to any child who can talk I try generally to talk not so differently as I would to an adult, except when I am playing a game which (typically, I fear) involves me playing the ridiculous adult and the child playing the sensible child, with me making up stories which become more and more far-fetched until the child intervenes and says "You're joking me!". Yes, some of us are sensible and some of us are crazy. But I would be mortified if you caught me talking about doggies or sweeties. I don't do that register of speech. It's talking down to the child and is quite unnecessary. It's not helpful to the child.

Why does that strange register of adult to child speech exist? Why is it sometimes continued into primary school Teacher Talk? I think there is an element of fear involved. Young children do indeed provoke fear: they run a fever and we are afraid they are going to die; they scream and we can't find a way to placate them and become afraid that we are in a situation we can't control; they run off in all directions, careless – or, sometimes, just seemingly careless

34

- of their personal safety. In this context, maybe it's the case that *doggies* and *sweeties* belong to a placatory register which adults address to Their Majesties the Babies.

I don't believe in Majesties. I do believe in children.

Futures Like the Past

HUMAN beings cannot be other than creatures of habit. They are obliged to create futures which are pretty much like their pasts. Habits can be changed, but only a few at a time and against a background of habits which remain intact. Changing a habit involves some kind of emotional and intellectual challenge, however minimal. You have to go outside your comfort zone and you have to learn something new. It's raising your game, it's stepping up to the plate, it's work.

Most of the time, human beings prefer their comfort zones and the absence of mental challenge to the work involved in change. Some human beings prefer to be comfortable and idle all the time. Inevitably, this often means settling for second best. Or worse. So people end up for very long - sometimes lifelong - periods in bad marriages and bad jobs, living in fuel-inefficient homes, driving fuel-inefficient cars, with their money going in and out of an account with a second-rate bank, taking a break from it all on cold and wet public holidays, being fed up with politicians. They grumble. Emotionally, it's a cheap alternative to change.

I opened my first bank account with Lloyds Bank in 1965 in order to pay in my university grant cheques. I stayed with Lloyds until the mid-1990s - let's say, thirty years. Lloyds was all right but not more than that. I found it hard to keep track of my finances and cheques did bounce. Their rates of interest on borrowing were almost certainly higher than ones I could have obtained elsewhere. A friend spent several years pointing out to me that I could change for the better. Eventually I moved to First Direct and I have never regretted it. Here was a bank where I could check the state of my account 24/7. I am never in trouble now. But there is something shocking about the way I resisted making a fairly simple change from one bank to another. And there are plenty of people who would never have done it. They would have stuck to their bank as if it was written into their marriage vows that they should do so. Mostly we live by the equivalent of marriage vows.

The UK has a pre-modern political system - a Ruritanian monarchy with the usual trappings of odd local rights and privileges (ownership of swans and such like); an unelected and completely corrupt second chamber; a first chamber designed to remind its Members of 19th century public schools. Those members have their own unbreakable habits - in the UK, the House of Commons, despite modest changes, remains submerged under fatuous rituals designed to create a backlog of real work and thus to stop as much change as possible. It is made tolerable to Members of Parliament only by the availability of large amounts of subsidised alcohol, recently revealed as the secret ingredient in the famous rowdiness of the House of Commons.

But even where politicians are open to change, they have to contend with the electorate's resistance. Voters are people who stand there, fold their arms and tell you that they always have done and always will do it THIS way. Urged to change, they will stamp their feet and cry, *Shan't! Can't! Won't!*

As a result, for example, the United Kingdom has no coherent system of weights and measures which everyone uses. For a number of years, the European Union tried to get us to Go Metric. But teachers had no intention of going metric (they didn't understand these foreign ideas) and market traders saw the chance to become Metric Martyrs, and like the pound sterling, wasn't it part of our Tradition and Heritage to have fourteen pounds to the stone and , er, eight stones to the hundredweight (which is not one hundred but one hundred and twelve pounds) and, your turn, how many hundredweights is it to the ton unless it's a short ton ….and so eventually the European Union gave up in the face of irredeemable stupidity. We were granted yet another opt-out. As a result, the UK is now pre-modern, with an incoherent jumble of systems in use.

Just visit any supermarket. Here you can find pints for some liquids, litres for others. Grams and kilos on one shelf, ounces and pounds on another. In Cornwall, maybe they still sell potatoes by the gallon. Weigh yourself on the bathroom scales, and some of us will use pounds and stones and some kilos. Medications are normally measured in milligrams and grams, millilitres and centilitres and not everyone understands what that all means so there are occasional disastrous results. Go to a fabric shop and you may find meters or you may find yards. Buy petrol and it's in litres, but distance measurement is in miles not kilometres. And, to rub it in, road signs show fractions of miles rather than decimal points of miles - as you approach the Channel Tunnel, you are counted down from two-thirds of a mile to one-third of a mile, a final flag-waving Work-That-Out-If -You-Can opt-out from new-fangled and, above all, foreign systems.

Two hundred years or more ago, as countries entered the

modern era, so they unified, simplified and extended the reach of systems of weights and measures. Local and highly particular traditions disappeared as did local currencies. The decimal system and the metric system are the expression of this move to the modern era, and their near-universal adoption is one of the enduring achievements of the French Revolution. It was a political achievement but the actual work was done by mathematicians and scientists of the first rank – Condorcet, Laplace, Lavoisier. They tried to work with British and American colleagues – Thomas Jefferson notable among them – but both those countries turned up their noses at what the French were proposing. It took Britain until 1971 to decimalise its currency and 1984 until the anomaly of a ½ penny coin was removed. But we still haven't made it into the modern era. Children learn how to use bits of different systems and none of them very well. They have no idea of how powerful a tool a unified system can be. They simply become good at bodging which is fine for a nation of bodgers. It's obtuse to expect children to be good at maths when their culture constantly tells them to muddle through with anything to do with numbers.

The moral is this: dysfunctional and, more generally, sub-optimal states of institutions and practices can persist indefinitely. They don't necessarily get eliminated any more than do pandas (who are terribly ill-adapted to their environment and generally miserable in consequence). All that happens is that people are generally miserable as they see their societies and economies grumbling and stumbling along, their politicians still aspiring to nothing more than an Opt Out from the modern world. But people won't do anything about it. They made their vows long ago.

Gender Formerly Known as Sex

I went online recently to check the status of my driving convictions. I was surprised to find at the head of the page which dealt with me the words "Gender: Male". Well, I have to say I never told them that. I am pretty sure that when I filled in their form however many decades ago I responded to a question which asked me for my "Sex" and that I answered "Male", which was truthful and true. If they had asked me for my "Gender", I am not sure I would have known what it was. The idea hadn't yet been imported. But why was it imported anyway? I have no real idea - I just guess that lots of people were reading the excellent, imported sociology textbook by Peter Berger and Thomas Luckmann *The Social Construction of Reality* (1966) and concluded that binary essentialist categories like Sex are Bad - because they imply that things exist which are not socially constructed - but binary non-essentialist, everything-is-a-social-construct categories like *Gender* are Good. Upper Seconds all round.

Gender is an adjectival rather than a nominal aspect of people's selves and it is rarely uncomplicated. Few people are as straightforwardly gendered (what is now called "cis-gendered") as is assumed by the bureaucrats whose imagination did not rise above deleting the word "Sex" and inserting the word "Gender". But just as few people are completely cis-gendered, few people are completely "trans-gendered". I doubt that there are many F people in transition to becoming M people who have Jeremy Clarkson as their target role model. As they start approaching that target, I feel they might decide to hang on to a bit of their F side.

We have always been taught that gender is distributed in a bi-polar way: plot people's gender on a statistical curve and there are big clusters of M people and F people on either side with only a few people in the middle. Over time and in different cultures, this may change. For example, I have read lots of Op Ed pieces telling me that over recent decades in my society boys have found it harder to develop (or been under pressure not to develop) + M masculine characteristics resulting in a "Crisis of Masculinity". Statistically, that would come out as a change in the shape of the distribution curve, reducing the M cluster on one side and creating a new bulge nearer the middle. In addition, if girls are under less pressure to stick to + F characteristics, then that would also create a bulge nearer the middle and we could then be on the way to what is called a normal curve of distribution (a Bell Curve - it looks like a church bell), with most people being bits of F and bits of M, regardless of sex, and clustering in the middle of the curve. If anything like that does happen, then people will begin to object to the gender binary boxes M and F.

But when big companies are castigated for not having a "Gender Balance" at top executive level no one would be amused if they adopted the following strategy:

Look, we're all men I know but, hey, some of us are less masculine than others – more feminine. Yeah? So why don't we start by scoring people for their

> *masculinity and their femininity? Like, you know,*
> *everyone says I am a "Good Listener" which must*
> *knock 10 points off my 100% Masculinity index. So*
> *why not credit those 10 points to the Female side of*
> *our Balance Sheet? That way, we at least make a start*
> *on changing the Gender Balance here. Yes, guys?*

No, guys. The truth is that your critics are talking anatomy. They don't like to say so, may even deny it, but anatomy is what they are talking about. Why should anatomy be so important? One reason is that it will remain an extremely powerful profiling tool for some basic things and quite powerful for other things until such time as we move to a normal curve of distribution for gender characteristics. You never need to be screened for prostate cancer if you tick the F box and you never need to be screened for ovarian cancer if you tick the M box. Athletic abilities also can be read off from your M or F profiling, which is why we have Men's and Women's events for most Olympic sports and tests to ensure people aren't cheating (which they do but that's another story). And so on, with the usefulness of the profiling declining as we move away from obvious ones like those I have just instanced. But until such time as most people have a significant mix of gender characteristics, it will be possible to profile for lots of things from anatomy alone: having driving convictions for speeding or annual expenditure on clothing, for example. In 2002, 83% of speeding convictions in the UK were picked up by men. In 2011, the Office of National Statistics records women spending £588 on their wardrobe and men £322.

Nothing more needs to be true for such profiling to be possible than the fact that societies set out to gender their new members – children – differentially according to their sex and that to, some considerable degree, they usually succeed. Parents and teachers (not to mention makers of children's toys and clothes) are huge enthusiasts for making sure that their M and F children are introduced to the right gender traits – hundreds of them - from very early in their lives. In some respects, it was less oppressively so forty years ago than it is now when everything is Pink or Blue, Girl or Boy. It wasn't quite so then. We can wish it otherwise and we can work to make it otherwise. That thought is only intelligible if you accept the basic distinction between Sex and Gender and don't conflate the two as has now been done on my driving licence.

*

Of course, the distinction between Sex and Gender has been known about for a very, very long time though sometimes I read things which tell me that someone discovered it last week. In England, the most intellectually serious daily newspaper is *The Financial Times.* On 28 November 2015, India Ross interviewed Jill Soloway, creator of the American TV series *Transparent* which has a transgender theme (I haven't seen it – no TV). They talk about gender issues and at the end Soloway says:

> *People will recognise that just because somebody is masculine, it doesn't mean they have a penis. Just because somebody's feminine, it doesn't mean they have a vagina. That's going to be the revolution over the next five years.*

India Ross adds:

> *I suggest that, even today, that's a fairly radical thing*
> *to say. She agrees ...*

I paused. When, if ever, has this "radical thing" not been recognised as true – and even platitudinously true?

Think, for example, of "cissy" and "tomboy". A cissy was a boy who displayed feminine tastes and traits, deemed unacceptable. A tomboy was a girl who displayed masculine tastes and traits, though sometimes these were treated more indulgently than cissy traits. To go back just sixty years, think of *To Kill a Mockingbird* which – among other things – belongs to a *genre* of tomboy novels. Go back a bit farther and you get to Jo March in Louisa May Alcott's *Little Women* (1868 – 69).

Both "cissy" and "tomboy" imply a fundamental distinction between sex and gender. Both recognise that sex and gender can be mismatched in a person. Neither supposes that cis-gendering (the neat matching of sex and gender) is inevitable, though as judgemental terms, they assume that cis-gendering is desirable. So maybe the revolution is simply to remove the judgemental aspect. No one will get called out as a cissy or laughed at as a tomboy. They will just be accepted. But didn't that also happen in the past?

Caring has been marked + *Feminine* in my culture and for a very long time. Let's go back a hundred years. In wars, like the unbelievably stupid and destructive First World War, there were male officers who distinguished themselves by *caring* for their men in terrible circumstances. This was regarded as admirable, not cissy.

Bravery has been marked + *Masculine* in my culture, also

44

for a very long time. But go back to 1838 and read the story of Grace Darling, a lighthouse keeper's daughter who assisted her father in the rescue of nine survivors from a shipwrecked steamer. This 23 year-old woman got marked + for *Bravery* (in fact, + + +). But no one dismissed her as a tomboy and several men who had never met her wrote seeking her hand in marriage. No one called her out for rowing the boat.

It is simply not true that the sex / gender distinction has ever been unclear to anyone, except perhaps to those who have been made to read Judith Butler's obscurantist *Gender Trouble* (1990). It is also - perhaps surprisingly - untrue that society has been consistently and remorselessly unwilling to recognise, accept, and even occasionally applaud, trans-gender characteristics as in the two examples instanced above.

Of course, its tolerance has never been whole-hearted and probably never consistent. But a flicker of tolerance can often be found. If we can nurture that flicker into something stronger, that will be a very good thing. But to do so it is both historically incorrect and politically unproductive to claim that we have just this last week invented something which will take us out of the Dark Ages once and for all. Lots of people like to be pioneers (maybe it's a + M thing); but most of the time, someone else got there already.

Curiously, the only situation in which Jill Soloway's claim makes sense is one where most people remain strongly cis-gendered, bunched at either end of the statistical curve but where a few (special?) people are allowed to cross the binary divide and join the other camp, with or without surgical intervention. That doesn't sound to me much like the social progress envisioned by mainstream feminists back in the 1970s who thought it was the fact of binary bunching itself which should be challenged. Feminists back then wanted women to be more assertive and men more caring, so that gendering became less Either – Or, more bunched in the middle, less a war between the Pinks and the Blues.

Hobbies & Hegel

I declare an interest in this subject: as a stamp dealer, I make a taxable income out of other people's hobbies. So I will have nothing disagreeable to say about them. But I do want to reclassify as hobbies some pursuits which usually have other labels like "academic research" (from which I used to derive a taxable income) and that will be the controversial bit.

Hobbies - pastimes - stand in contrast to work. They may absorb much time and energy, but they are not the way you earn your living. This does not exclude that, at the end of the day - or sooner - a hobby may increase someone's assets; some collections turn into very valuable things. But not all hobbies are asset-building: bird-watching isn't.

Hobbies contrast with work in another way. They may be pursued passionately and arouse passions, they may be intellectually demanding, but normally they do not involve the kind of emotional demands made by a job or even by life in general. They are relaxation. They take your mind away from work. They give you something else to think about. Thus is explained the surgeon who collects stamps.

Indeed, if something does engage the same emotions and strains as work or everyday life then we tend not to call it a hobby. Back in 1967, I was a twenty year old politically engaged student doing a summer vacation job as a researcher. In conversation one day, my boss called political activism "a hobby". That was cynicism with a grain of truth: getting involved in politics can indeed be a way of passing the time. The time would have passed anyway. But not so quickly. Interestingly, I have never forgotten the remark.

But political activism isn't really a hobby: it's too close to the everyday world with its demands and unpredictability, its challenges and defeats. And it matters. You might say that the whole *point* of a hobby is that it isn't about making the world a better place or indeed having any effect on the world. A hobby isn't a hobby if its absence from the world would make a difference. A hobby can die out and the world goes on much as before.

In the fifth edition of his *Fruit Manual*, published in 1884, the famous horticulturalist Robert Hogg lists several hundred varieties of gooseberry. The large number is owing to the fact that in parts of northern England, growing gooseberries for competitive exhibition was a popular 19th century working class male hobby (pursuit, pastime). Hogg duly records after the name of each gooseberry variety the name of the man who introduced it: Freedom (Moore), Garibaldi (Walton), Independent (Brigg), Pastime (Bratherton), Railway (Livesey), Sheba Queen (Crompton) … Unlike pigeon fancying, gooseberry fancying - which came with its own Craft mysteries ("Table by which the approximate weight of Gooseberries may be ascertained by measurement with the callipers" Hogg, page 366) - is all but lost and forgotten. The world may be a bit poorer but not at a loss.

That is why for some people hobbies are a waste of time. Serious people don't have hobbies. They have better things to do. Even when they are absorbed in a relaxing activity, like watching a play, they are actually doing something better: improving their minds. This move to take something out of the mere "Hobby" category and write it up as something worthier then becomes the basis for many assumptions, among them that the State should subsidise theatre ticket prices. I suppose it's one of the main reasons that I have never really made it into the middle class, that I can see no more reason why the State should subsidise theatre tickets than tickets to football matches or rock concerts. It's too much like arguing that the Government should step in and subsidise the price of *Premier Cru* wines so that the middle classes don't have to fork out so much to afford a taste. It would be an argument for a big subsidy if going to the theatre or the opera helped stop you sending people to the gas chambers but that argument, unfortunately, is no longer available.

*

Recently, I took down from my shelves a book I bought maybe twenty or thirty years ago but had never read: *Hegel's Aesthetics* in the fat two volume translation by Sir Malcolm Knox. I made a start on this classic and difficult work. Knox was a University professor of philosophy and then a university Principal. He did Hegel translations during his career and he continued in retirement: he retired in 1966 and the *Aesthetics* was published in 1975. His work had become his retirement hobby and none the worse for that.

My controversial proposal, promised at the outset, is that much of the work done in universities within government-funded Humanities departments ought to be re-classified as

Hobby. Editing classical texts, translating poetry, compiling bibliographies, writing commentaries and biographies - these are splendid hobbies for people with demanding professional lives and for those who have retired from them. In the past they often were. They provided intellectual challenge and required dedication - often enough obsessive dedication - but they also provided relaxation - escape - from the demands either of careers or ordinary chores. There is no pressing reason why such activities should be funded by the State and jobs for life made out of them. The world might indeed be a richer place if we had to rely on them being pursued as hobbies.

That's a big claim and needs some expansion. One of the reasons I make it is that I have always had doubts about what universities actually did and achieved, even though several were very kind to me. If you take the long view, universities have rarely encouraged scientific enquiry or tolerance of different opinions. Often enough, they have not been so very different from overtly theological seminaries which don't even pretend to value Science or Toleration. Both universities and seminaries recruit from the same age groups and – until very, very recently – they have only been interested in recruiting those biologically sexed as male. The teachers have been even more exclusively male, often with a requirement of celibacy or (what used to be called) bachelorhood. In the long view, the history of a university like Oxford makes you wonder why we bother. If instead of picking on Oxford, you looked at an average university in France or Italy, the case against would be overwhelming. In the past, there were people – women most obviously - who were barred from all these places but who did scholarly work of far more enduring value than those spare sons provided with a university living and lodgings. George Eliot's translations of the philosopher of religion, Ludwig Feuerbach, are still in use.

It's easy to think that things have changed and it is not like the bad old days. I'm not so sure and I'm not so sure it could be otherwise. Ironically, it is in those countries and cultures which appear most attached to the values of truth and tolerance that sceptical ("deconstructionist"), relativist (anti – "humanist") and anti-realist (anti – "essentialist") theories have been in vogue among university teachers and students of the humanities who then – unable to appeal to any notions of truth or right – substitute pursed-lip disapproval or outrage for any kind of considered judgement on the ill-considered opinions or misguided views of others around the table.

I'm thinking about places like Literature Departments in British and American universities, bursting at the seams with young seminarians anxiously working out what they must say to please their professors, treating them (sometimes with good reason) as immensely vain people who have to be flattered. It's not just vanity which is a problem. There are still lots of professors who just aren't very good at what they are supposed to profess and whose insecurity surely derives from a fear of being found out. That, I think, is one of the roots of the obscurity which is passed off in academic work as profundity when it is no more than a literary trope designed to disguise the fact that, really, you have nothing to say which can be formulated fairly rigorously and at least moderately clearly. It is not surprising that academic journals which publish this stuff have been hoaxed, the most famous example provided by an article of consummate absurdity successfully submitted in 1996 to a journal *Social Text* by a Professor of Physics, Alan Sokal, and since much discussed.

The philosopher of science, Paul Feyerabend, paints a similar picture of the humanities when describing (in a 1967 essay) the work of the physicist Felix Ehrenhaft in 1940s Vienna and a style of lecturing which Feyerabend later made his own and to great effect:

*His method of teaching was unusual also. It was quite possible, in physics, in mathematics, in astronomy to interrupt the lecturer and to ask for the clarification of a doubtful point (the situation was very different in philosophy and in the humanities where many lecturers rejoiced in giving sermons and where interruption was almost an act of sacrilege). But Ehrenhaft **challenged** us to criticize him and criticized **us** for just **listening** to what he had to say. I can still remember him exploding at one point and shouting at us: "Are you dumb? Are you stupid? Or do you really agree with everything I say?" The question was quite justified for there were large chunks to swallow...* [emphases in the original]

Of course, the kinds of science in which a good Literature department could engage are not the same as those which are deployed by the Physics department. As places where Texts are read, the essential discipline for a literature student is the ability to pay attention to the Text (which someone may have had to edit for such use). From there, it's possible to go on to respond to and interpret it in an indefinite number of ways – as Comic, Tragic or Pornographic; as the Expression of a personality, as the (witting or unwitting) vehicle for an Ideology, as belonging to a Tradition, as embodying a distinctive Voice, as in (acknowledged or unconscious) Dialogue with other Texts – and so on and so forth. As you respond and interpret, so the Text itself may re-focus: you notice things you didn't notice the first time round. So interpretation has no obvious end (as the deconstructionists would agree), though it may approach it asymptotically - by which I mean that sometimes we exhaust the plausible possibilities and supposed new interpretations are just arbitrary and forced. What I have just said about "Texts" applies equally if you change that word to "Paintings".

I think we might get better work done in the humanities without the seminaries. If people want to read books together, there can be evening classes, book clubs, residential weekends, and now, of course, internet forums. We don't really need the big bureaucracies, the professional career structure and the clubs of like-minded people giving each other a leg up. The last is a definite disaster zone. Hobbyists come in all shapes and sizes; university lecturers less so.

In recent years, some of the best books I have read are the work of very clever people who haven't followed the career path into university teaching but, instead, have become political activists or bankers or serious journalists. But they have made research and writing their hobby. I have in mind books like Liaquat Ahamed's *The Lords of Finance* (2009) a superb book about American and European central banking from 1914 to the 1930s written by someone who describes himself as a professional investment manager. If he wanted, he could get a Professorship anywhere on the strength of his book; maybe he will. And - this is a note to readers working in the financial sector – what he has accomplished was probably more satisfying than snorting cocaine, which in London currently wins out every Friday night (the evidence is in the sewers next day).

I will misuse a tripartite classification from an essay by Roland Barthes, himself a rather reluctant and uncomfortable academic [see the Endnote]. *Writers* have no future as writers if they can't write. *Intellectuals* need ideas - a vision even - or else no one will listen. But *Professors* can advance in their careers and hang their hats on a decent pension though quite unable to write and pretty much devoid of ideas. They have the power to make generations of students labour over unreadable and soon-to-be-demoted books which in a free world would be left unread and never promoted in the first place. I think *Hobbyists* might sometimes serve us better.

*

Endnote:

For the academic year 1971 – 72, Barthes offered a lecture series on the history of semiology. The École Pratique des Hautes Études, aware of his popularity, assigned him a public theatre. There was an evening production running and the static set on stage included a sign with the words "Le Petit Cirque". Rather than stand at the front of the stage and lecture, Barthes installed himself behind a plain desk and sat on a hard chair. During the second or third lecture, someone in the gallery audience got up and denounced him for still thinking in Binary terms when the world had move on to Ternary, etc etc. Ludicrous, of course, but not for Barthes who never returned to the theatre. He moved himself to an ordinary seminar room, kept semi-secret so that the audience size dwindled down from a couple of hundred to twenty or thirty. He was my director of studies, so I was one of those who kept going.

Ingratitude & Disloyalty

SOMEONE was talking about cats and dogs and remarked on the ingratitude of cats. I think this is probably why I am at ease with them. In contrast, dogs make me uncomfortable. They are smelly and sloppy and jump all over you (reminding you of the time when you were attacked by one) but there's more to it than that. They just like humans too much. It's not natural.

Gratitude makes me uncomfortable. There is a spontaneous, uncomplicated kind of gratitude which expresses itself and then disappears. I am fine with that. But I am always afraid that gratitude will get mixed up with guilt and consequently endure longer than it should. It becomes an expression of loyalty and I am not very comfortable with that either. Loyalty usually comes mixed up with guilt or is used to dump guilt on the object of loyalty. I don't do loyalty very well, either to people or institutions. I still think it's a fault of character but I want to persuade you that there are reasons for thinking that lack of loyalty is maybe not such a big one. When other people pull Loyalty on you - either their own loyalty or your own lack of it - it's to make you feel bad. The world is full of Loyal Wives and Loyal Husbands who have burnished their loyalty into a powerful weapon of attack. The other party is left cowering.

Servants are expected to be loyal to their employer,

especially if that's a Prince Charles or a Princess Diana. The servants' loyalty is necessary if the employers are to conduct their affairs and trysts and intrigues without risk of discovery. This kind of loyalty is a one-way street which the powerful expect of the powerless. It's really obedience by another name. It was a disloyal manservant who leaked the little-known information that England's last Hanging Judge, Lord Chief Justice Goddard, orgasmed into his pin striped trousers as he handed down death sentences.

British politics is characterised by tribal loyalties. Young men must choose their party no later than Oxford and the Bullingdon Club and stick with it through thick and thin if they are to have any chance of rising to the top. Only the prospect of imminent foreign invasion in 1940 allowed the party-hopper, Winston Churchill, to become Prime Minister - which he did on the back of the disloyalty of over 70 Conservative MPs withdrawing support from their own government following a string of military set-backs. That act of disloyalty is crystallised forever in the image of the Tory MP, Leopold Amery, calling across to the Labour benches as its Deputy Leader, Arthur Greenwood, rose to his feet: *Speak for England, Arthur!* For such disloyalty, we have profound reason to be grateful. But it's not a feeling we should want to experience very often.

*

Children are naturally ungrateful and this is a healthy trait. The job of children is to exhaust you, take your love and your money, and then fuck off. They don't owe you any gratitude. If they still love you or at least quite like you after the way you have brought them up, that's surely wonderful and as good as it ought to get.

Children are not insurance policies against your old age, though that is how they have often been treated in many cultures around the world and still are. I always find myself quite angered by this. My mother - as the youngest of seven - ended up with the job of staying at home to care for her ageing mother and, in turn, rather hoped that I would stay at home and keep her company. It may have been a close run thing that I didn't. That may explain the recollection I still have of watching Shohei Imamura's *The Ballad of Narayama* (1983) at Brighton's Duke of York's cinema. It's a beautiful and deeply moving film, set in the past, about a poor rural Japanese society in which the elderly are, by custom and tradition, exposed to die on the bleak mountains when they reach the age of seventy. The central drama is between a mother, who believes in the custom, and her son who resists his duty, which is to carry her on her final journey to the mountain. At one point, to make the bogus case that she is becoming useless, the mother smashes her mouth against a stone ledge in order to render herself a toothless old woman. The Japanese film resonates with elements in Western culture. Think of "Greater love hath no man than this ..." and its exemplar, Captain Oates, marching to his death in the snow.

In both Japan and the West, life expectancy has risen dramatically in just a short period and continues to rise. It places strains on government budgets, obliged to fund pension payments for many more years than was ever foreseen and to support expensive care for the elderly frail. The elderly frail are those in no state either to seek to prolong their lives or to shorten them. But those in a pre-frail state have some choices. Occasionally, they refuse further medical treatment. Occasionally, they live it up and do all the things they have been advised not to. In other words, they do not strive officiously to keep themselves alive. But very rarely do they actually commit suicide though sometimes they starve themselves.

People grow old at different rates and their circumstances are different: there are now lots of men in their seventies with quite young children to care for. But as a general rule, governments should not strive to keep alive the elderly, especially when their quality of life is deteriorating irreversibly. Budgets need to be finite for medical treatment and for care. There should be no funding for research aimed at extending life expectancy. If done intelligently and sensitively, the results would be better than an uncritical policy of keeping everyone alive for as long as possible. There comes a point when it is time to show a bit of ingratitude.

Judging by Appearances

LONG before political correctness arrived, we were told not to judge by appearances; not to judge a book by its cover. As a result, people qualified opinions by saying "Judging by appearances ..." to signal that they stood willing to be corrected. Yet, from another perspective, social life would become impossible if we did not routinely believe people and that means accepting the appearances they present to us. Unfortunately, those appearances may be intended to deceive or mislead. But finding out that someone is lying will often require a level of intrusiveness not generally acceptable. It is not only police of various kinds but also social scientists and social critics who have to face up to that problem; they are supposed to seek the truth, not prove that they are polite or well-meaning.

There was once a stock literary character, the elderly spinster or widow living in "genteel poverty". The money had run out but she tried to keep up appearances, deceiving the world into thinking that there was more in her purse than there really was. Had a social scientist investigating income poverty passed through and asked her how she was doing, she would have replied "Very Well, Thank You", and that would have been the end of the discussion. She would not have welcomed further questioning and so her poverty could only be imagined, as indeed it was – but by novelists rather than social scientists.

The opposites of the genteel spinster are all those people who plead poverty when they aren't poor. Often, they have a plausible case because their "official" incomes are poverty incomes. But sometimes those incomes have hidden supplements. Crime, work in the black economy, windfalls, extended family support and inheritances all boost people's standards of living. They may provide unreliable and intermittent boosts to income, but that is not a reason to ignore them. Some people get through their whole life on a series of windfalls. There are windfalls from Premium Bonds and the Lottery. When Premium Bonds were introduced in 1956, my paternal grandmother presented me with one. Just one. I still have it somewhere. But if you manage to buy a few thousand Premium Bonds, then you will have tax-free windfalls from time to time which don't show up as "Interest on Savings". It's one of the things my father relied on. As he got older, he also had a striking appearance of poverty. He lived in a caravan, one that looked like a caravan not a Park Home. Lottery wins are also tax free. I realise that lotteries are basically a tax on the poor, but even a modest lottery win can temporarily boost the income of an extended family. Most inheritances are also tax free and even poor people get them sometimes. They can provide an enormous boost to a family's fortunes.

Only if you probe behind the appearances most of us present to the world can you explain things like the ability of so many families with modest incomes to come up with staggering sums of money to blow on weddings. (Somewhere I read that the more you spend, the sooner the divorce). If you are going to make a serious study of inner city deprivation or rural poverty or the struggling elderly, you need to factor in all the things I have mentioned. In this way, you will identify both those who are not so poor as they appear and those who really are poor because they have no access to hidden supplements.

Turn now from the poorer to the richer. There are those who are willing to admit to affluence but who are in reality rather more than affluent, indeed, wealthy. There have always been very rich people whose lives are outwardly modest and occasionally mean. The wealth is kept discreetly hidden in bank accounts, bank vaults and sometimes just in cupboards and attics. Income flows are opaque. In my lifetime, I have known quite a few people who had what used to be called "Private Incomes" but though it's unusual to meet someone who doesn't want to disclose their salary, I have never met anyone who has told me the annual value of their private income. Not one. Jane Austen would have been greatly inconvenienced were she alive now; in her time, everyone who mattered could be ranked by their private income. Tax officials often do not find hidden wealth and income (sometimes aren't even looking) and neither do social scientists. It's easy to suppose that what we are dealing with is greed but sometimes it is simply carelessness. That is also difficult to investigate.

In my current line of work there is a familiar enough career pattern. We are all sole traders, mostly start young, generally ignore the age of retirement and keep trading until our health gives out. At any provincial stamp fair, you can find sitting behind a table dealers in their eighties. Traditionally, stamp dealers are a bit like booksellers who carry very high stocks relative to turnover. Sometimes stock accumulates without planning. It happens like this (and since 95% of dealers are male, I will for once write about "he"). A stamp dealer buys – with a bit of luck - one hundred identical stamps in a sheet for £100. He breaks up the sheet and sells the first ten stamps at £10 each and gets his money back – such 1000% mark ups do often enough occur. Then he sells another ten at £5 each which contributes to his trading expenses – tables at stamp fairs, travelling, office costs and so on – and leaves him a bit of money for himself. Then he gets bored with this batch of stamps and puts the remaining eighty in a drawer and forgets about them. Occasionally, he may ferret one out if pressed for a copy. But the money he got back on the first sheet, he has long since turned into another and different sheet, and so on repeatedly. This can and does go on for decades, filling up first drawers, then cupboards, then garages. The dealer never looks particularly affluent and certainly not wealthy. He drives a second hand car and dresses badly. He grumbles about the NHS waiting list he is on and when it is suggested that he goes Private replies that he hasn't got the money. He supplements his pension at table-top fairs, selling off bits and pieces from the vast hoard at home. Then he dies. His executors send the contents of the drawers, cupboards and garages straight to the municipal tip (this happens) or else they call in a firm of auctioneers to take it all away. The auctioneers sort it out roughly into boxes – they don't have the time or expertise to make more effort – and sell it at maybe 10 or 20% of its retail value and the executors end up with a million pounds. It happens and it is a nice way of refuting the idea that all businesses are rational, profit maximising entities. It's also the kind of thing that a social scientist may miss, notably because there is a narrative to be discovered which covers decades and which won't show up if you ask, "What is your weekly income?"

The stamp dealer's hidden wealth is not so very different to the wealth which accumulates in country houses in the form of furniture, silverware, paintings and so on. It is only when someone dies and the valuers for probate go in that it emerges just how many silver spoons the drawers of a country house can accommodate.

So here we have wealth which is not about greed but, at worst, about hoarding. The hoarding may not be patholog-ical, just a side-effect of laziness and carelessness: the stamp dealer looks at the contents of his garage and sighs, "I can't be bothered any more". The widow in the country house looks and sighs, "It's all too much for me now" – and it is, that's the problem. The way their world appears to the casual observer or the uninquisitive social scientist can be very misleading. You can't judge a book by its cover; you have to read it.

Kingdom of Ruritania, Kingdom of Yugoslavia

THE 29th April 2011 was a public holiday in Ruritania. Ruritanian public holidays were not quite the same as public holidays in other countries. For one thing, they were called Bank Holidays. For another, the government merely *advised* employers to lock out their workers; it did not compel them. From time to time, the government added extra days to the annual list of public holidays. The 29th April 2011 was added to the list by Mr Cameron, one of the last Prime Ministers of Ruritania, so that everyone whose employer followed the advice could stay at home and watch television.

The Monarchy was mounting a big television spectacular, the wedding of its Prince William of Wales - second in line to the throne - to a commoner, Miss Middleton, who had been deemed acceptable as a baby maker. (The assessment proved correct; she produced healthy babies thus securing - had all gone to plan - the Ruritanian Royal Line for the next hundred years).

The youngish couple, who had met at University while studying Art History, drew up a very large Guest List for their televised wedding - or, more accurately, had it drawn up for them by the Department of Royal Protocol. Included were:

Crown Prince Alexander and Crown Princess Katherine of Yugoslavia
The Princess Elizabeth of Yugoslavia

In 1941, the Kingdom of Yugoslavia was occupied by German, Italian, Hungarian and Bulgarian forces who divided up the country with Croatia notable for a particularly murderous regime headed by Ante Pavelić.

Opposed to the Occupation, King Peter II of Yugoslavia and his government went into exile. The King arrived in London, the Ruritanian capital, in June 1941 joining several other exiled governments based there. And as with other governments-in-exile, it was supposed to direct anti-Nazi and anti-fascist resistance in the occupied homeland. Some of these exiled governments were very effective – the Polish, for example, which among other things provided 145 of the 2927 pilots who were officially recognised as "The Few" who flew in what was called the Battle of Britain.

But by 1943, intercepts of German military radio traffic (the ULTRA intercepts, one of Ruritania's great war time successes) showed fairly unambiguously that Yugoslav Royalist forces (known as the Chetniks) were acting independently of their own government-in-exile and had for the most part allied themselves with the Germans and Italians. They were more or less exclusively engaged in attacks on the occupiers' main enemies and their own political rivals, Tito's anti-fascist, anti-Nazi and pro-Communist Partisans.

It wasn't really King Peter's fault; he was a very young man and in exile. The Royalists had been divided in their attitudes towards Nazism and fascism even before the Axis powers invaded, with some wanting to welcome them. But as a result of the Intelligence information he was receiving, the charismatic Ruritanian Prime Minister, Winston Churchill, withdrew support from the Royalist Chetniks and thenceforth gave exclusive support to the Partisans. Tito's headquarters became home to distinguished Allied agents like the Special Operations Executive's Fitzroy Maclean, personally selected for the job by Churchill in a famous Memorandum of July 1943.

Maclean did raise with Churchill the likelihood that this support would mean that, after the war, Yugoslavia would become a Communist country. Maclean writes in his Memoirs:

> *The Prime Minister's reply resolved my doubts.*
> *'Do you intend', he asked, 'to make Yugoslavia your*
> *home after the war?'*
> *'No, Sir' I replied.*
> *'Neither do I'*

After end-of-war elections, Yugoslavia's Constituent Assembly deposed King Peter II on 29 November 1945 and declared a Republic. The victorious Allies were happy to recognise it and for most of the next thirty five years enjoyed at least reasonable relations with Tito's communist Yugoslavia. Yugoslavia became a popular holiday destination for Ruritanian tourists. Then under the far-right nationalist Slobodan Milošević, things went from bad to worse.

With the secession of Montenegro in 2006, Yugoslavia finally ceased to exist. Instead - as Ruritania's citizens discovered from the so-called "Eurovision" song contests – it disintegrated into Bosnia-Herzegovina, Croatia, the Former-Yugoslav-Republic of Macedonia, Kosovo, Montenegro, Slovenia and – finally – the rump state of Serbia.

None of this - literally none of this - had been noticed in Ruritania's royal palaces. Nothing that had happened in the last seventy years impinged on its conviction that the

Kingdom of Yugoslavia still existed with Alexander its Crown Prince, entitled to three seats at the royal wedding. Some historians attribute the fall of the Ruritanian Kingdom to such dissociations from reality.

Lipstick Semiotics

THERE are still places *where* lipstick can get you in trouble and once there were places *when* it would. The trouble could be pretty serious. This yields a first pair of concepts relevant to semiotic analysis: Place (Where) and Time (When). An analysis which overlooks the *When* risks being anachronistic, projecting on to another time something which is only now true. An analysis which overlooks the *Where* risks some kind of *–centrism*, projecting on to another place what is only true here. Here and Now (where I'm writing from) lipstick only gets *some* people into trouble. More on that in a moment. Where I'm writing from, here and now, is nearly fifty years on from when I first encountered the word "Semiotics" and its synonym "Semiology" and read the books of Ferdinand de Saussure, Roland Barthes and others before turning or returning to other approaches to the study of signs, in the work of theorists like Chomsky and the English philosophers J L Austin and H P Grice.

Back to lipstick. Putting on lipstick is an *act* (usually performed with the help of a mirror, sometimes done quickly, sometimes carelessly …) which results in an appearance or inscription, *painted lips*. There is another semiotic distinction here, one between *doing something* and *what is done*. If in a burning building I shout "Fire!", what I am doing is most likely *warning* other people by means of shouting the word "Fire!", the meaning of which word guides my hearers to look for fire and run from it rather than, say, from water or an escaped python. But there could have been no fire and shouting "Fire!" I could have been playing a practical joke, trying to make you run when there was no fire to run from. (Do that on an aeroplane and you go to jail). In both cases, there is a constant element in what is done – the shouting of "Fire!" - and a variable element in what I do – warn you or play a joke on you.

In semiotic terms, this is about the distinction between the *pragmatics* of something done and the *semantics* of whatever is used (words, images, make-up) to do it. The pragmatics of what is done may, in the final analysis, reduce to my intentions in doing something but there is philosophical debate about whether, in the final analysis, such a reduction will (always) go through. It doesn't much matter here. The *semantics* of what is done is what dictionaries try to capture though they have a hard time of it because meaning depends on use or usage and may even be reducible to it. Again, there is philosophical disagreement. No matter: ordinary dictionaries will continue to tell us what words mean and make-up dictionaries how the meaning of painted lips varies with colour and style.

Those who cause you trouble over lipstick may have either pragmatics or semantics in mind when they come after you, though they may not be entirely clear whether it's one or the other or both. Imagine, for example, that – *somewhere, somewhen* - they infer from the presence of lipstick on your lips (from the *sign*) that you intend by means of that sign to signal sexual availability, which they promptly tell you is punishable. They also tell you that the sign is meant to arouse sexual desire in others who see you, which they tell you is also punishable. Both are accusations of intent, about the relationship between you as agent and your painted lips as the sign you have created. Suppose you deny both offences and say "It's just lipstick". It doesn't cut it. They shake their heads and, say, "Yeah, that's what people say to us when we catch them using the word "Nigger". Do you think that's just a word?"

You may try again. "But it's just lip balm!" "But it's not even red!" In both instances, a new semiotic category has been invoked, the idea of a *semantic field*. If you claim that it's lip balm not lipstick, you are trying to move the inscription on your lips from one semantic field to another, rather like claiming that it's not chalk but cheese. It may work, but it may require a ruling from a deputy head teacher if you are an English school girl or a religious official if you are a girl in a Muslim culture.

In semiotic contexts, such rulings are attempts to eliminate uncertainties which surround the creation of meaning in everyday life. The ruling is made, "Lip balm does not count as lipstick" and you get off. Then some smart entrepreneur starts marketing pink lip balm and the ruling has to change: "Colourless lip balms do not count as lipstick, but coloured ones do". This can go on, will require school governor and religious council meetings, and helps keep everyone in business. (Ask Google if Muslims can wear lipbalm and 250 000 results appear; ask about lipstick and 500 000).

Suppose instead of offering the Lip Balm Defence, you say, "But it's not even Red!" This opens up even bigger business possibilities, this time for what used to be called casuistry, which is still a useful word; it refers to the organised practice of trying to settle particular cases or disputes from more general principles which are agreed on both sides. In this new defence, you have made a move which concedes the general principle that lipstick can be used to signal or provoke something sexual, but you then qualify this by suggesting that in *the semantic field of lipstick colours as you understand them* there are indeed colour shades which send sexual signals (you have nominated Red lipsticks) but that yours isn't one of them. Your case is different. You point out that your lipstick is Black, and simply signals that you are a Goth, and surely they know that?

Unfortunately, your tormentors have been on the Internet and they point out that though it would once have been true that *black lipstick* was used only by those intending to signal themselves as Goths, this is no longer the case. The semantic field has shifted and black lipstick is now (2015 according to the forums) simply a fashionable colour, but no different to red in its sexual colouring. And with some satisfaction, your tormentors say, "You wouldn't want us to be anachronistic, would you?" Your move. "How was I supposed to know? I only look at Goth things on the Internet".

Actually, this set-up is a bit unfair because it is usually the tormentors who stumble over changing semantic fields. In schools, they are never able to keep up with the changing semantic fields of skirt lengths, tie knots, shoe styles and, most difficult of all, hair styles. A week in hair styles is a long time and schools can't cope with that pace of change. But as schools discovered long ago, the way out of a lot of time spent on casuistry is just to impose rules, grit your teeth and stick to them through whatever happens to the relevant semantic field. Lipstick? You just ban it and that's the end of the matter, you hope.

71

What that shows, perhaps inadvertently, is that you are working with what semioticians call a *binary distinction*, which in this case has a second dual character. First off, there is what looks like a simple *Plus / Minus* binary: lips with lipstick opposed to lips without lipstick. But one of the binaries is *privileged*: Minus Lipstick is privileged and the privilege connects to another binary, *Nature / Culture*. The "No Lipstick" rule inevitably implies that lips in a natural state are to be preferred to lips in a cultural state, perhaps for everyone perhaps just for some (females under 18, females under 16, females under …, all males). But, anyway, Nature Good and Culture Bad. Bad move. The world's most skilful casuists will now take you by storm:

Miss, Does that mean we mustn't shave our arm pits?
Miss, Does that mean we mustn't use under arm deodorant? Miss, Can I pluck my eyebrows or not?
Miss, Can I shave my legs?

This is fun and it is tempting to go on, but I want to generalise it before returning to the casuistry. This involves introducing one of the original semiotic distinctions.

*

All societies have different rules for Boys and Girls, many of the differences weird and wonderful. Those rules (conventions, traditions, norms …) co-exist in what linguists who follow Saussure call a *synchronic state* which is simply a cross-sectional or static state from which time has been eliminated. A grammar of a language is the paradigm example of something suitable for synchronic study, an approach which takes an object out of time as if it was a mathematical object.

But the grammar or other apparatus extracted for study actually evolves in real time history, often in ways which are extremely complicated and hard to disentangle. Historical linguistics, the *diachronic* study of language change, is not for the faint hearted: study language as it changes in history and you immediately have to take account of hundreds of variables at work. Historical lipstick studies face the same problem. Among other things, they have to take on this question of what is this thing called Nature.

What I mean is this. Though it is true that a binary between Nature and Culture operates in the discussion of things like Make Up, the category *Nature* is itself changeable through time and always incorporates acceptance of some kinds and some level of what I will call *Body Maintenance* into its concept of Nature. Over very long periods of time, centuries and decades , there are shifts in what I will call - using a concept which Roland Barthes applied to literary writing - the *Degree Zero* of Body Maintenance. The Degree Zero of Body Maintenance is moveable and moves.

To be less opaque: (nearly?) all Cultures expect you to wash and do not see this as an offence against Nature or even as non-natural. But what changes over time is *what counts as washing*. Does it mean one bath a year (which I associate with Queen Elizabeth the First) or one bath a week (which I guess Elizabeth the Second exceeds)? Does it mean a daily shower? I guess no one is going to declare a daily shower "unnatural" or "sexual provocation".

Likewise, at some point, cleaning your teeth and then cleaning them regularly got incorporated into the Body

Maintenance which cultures expect of their members. So today, having bad breath is a sure way of losing friends and influence over people. So is dandruff which modern hair washing regimes have more or less eliminated (when I was a child, dandruff was endemic). None of this is counted as against Nature; indeed, not having dandruff is – one might say - more *Degree Zero* than having it.

What one might call rising expectations about Body Maintenance does mean, for example, that there were people in the past who were regarded as odd or eccentric or vain or religiously suspect because they exceeded the Degree Zero expectations but who today nearly everyone would actually find grubby and smelly. Three hundred years ago if you changed your underwear every day, that would have been really weird; not today.

But these rising expectations are not an uncomplicated good thing and that is partly because they have often imposed differential requirements on boys and girls. So at least up until now, it is not part of Degree Zero body maintenance for boys and men to shave their armpits or their legs, nor to pluck their eyebrows. However, use of deodorant probably is part of the Degree Zero if you are otherwise inclined to smell of stale sweat. In contrast, Degree Zero expectations for girls and women are more demanding (of time and effort) which is one reason why they are regarded as unfair (which is what *sexist* would mean here). There was at least a short time in which the expectations were more balanced – the time when boys and men were expected to shave their facial hair daily unless they grew a full beard (which itself might be forbidden – in my secondary school days, boys were not allowed to wear beards though some were fully capable of growing them).

But that Degree Zero expectation on men has now lapsed, driven by the men's fashion industry. On the female side, there was one fairly recent (1970s – 1980s) failure to raise the Degree Zero – the attempt to introduce vaginal deodorants encountered very widespread resistance and, as I understand things, must now be counted as a failure.

In very general terms, make up can be seen as Surplus to a culture's conception of the essential (non-negotiable, Degree Zero) Body Maintenance for which it was once claimed that Cleanliness is next to Godliness. It is, of course, a huge surplus embracing cosmetic attention to hair, eyes, mouth, skin, nails … and so on. Each element in that surplus, together with the overall structure, can be studied semiotically and both synchronically and diachronically. In every case one can ask questions about intent (the pragmatics) which itself can be separated into self-directed and other-directed. One can also try to map the very complex semantic fields through which intent is navigated or conveyed. And then there is the structuring and manipulation of both intent and semantics by a worldwide, multibillion cosmetics industry. And to top it off and back to where we started from, there is the Make Up Police. I think you will agree, they cannot possibly do their job without Ph. Ds.

Macadamised

IT'S always rained a lot in the United Kingdom and now it rains even more. When I am sidestepping pavement puddles and driving along main roads sheeted with water, I keep thinking that civilisations in decline forget how to use - or cannot be bothered to use - the technologies which once made them great. Think of what happened to Britain when the Romans left and it was immediately as if central heating technology had never been invented; according to Winston Churchill in *A History of the English Speaking Peoples*, Britain knew neither central heating or hot baths for 1500 years, the people shivering and smelly.

In school, and quite young, we did the Agricultural and Industrial Revolutions. We learnt about advances in civil engineering which introduced an era of road improvement and we knew the names of Thomas Telford (1757-1834) and John Macadam (1756 - 1836), both Scotsmen. The latter gave us the word "Tarmac", shortened from "Tarmacadam". I can still remember the diagrams, though I don't have the exercise books any more. The basic idea was something like this: you built up the road with small stones and at the same time you *cambered* the road, so that water ran to the sides where it could be drained into ditches. Then you applied tar to the surface. Unlike the old mud roads, the

Macadamised road would remain passable in the wettest weather. In the context of growth of industry and trade, and until railways became widespread, it was an innovation of direct benefit to business which helps explain why Macadam's ideas were taken up. In towns, those ideas had the same advantage: water from cambered streets would flow towards gutters and from there would be channeled into drains. As a final flourish of civic pride and common sense, pavements could be gently sloped so that they too drained into the gutters.

All this we have forgotten.

In towns, our roads and pavements are dug up endlessly by utility firms and councils. They employ the same firms: Bodger and Sons, Bodger and Daughters, Bodger and Bodger. None of them has heard of road cambering or water runoff. Or if they have, they don't want to know. They want the money. Not so many years ago, cumbersome council vehicles dropped great nozzles into street drains to suck out leaves and other debris and thus ensure that the drains were fit for purpose. Now we have privatised drains and no cumbersome vehicles. Drains are blocked: when it rains the water may run towards the drains but there it simply overflows and spreads out into those great ponds of water which buses drive through.

On the main roads and motorways, large private companies extract from the Exchequer millions for maintenance. But Bodger and Bodger Plc has never heard of cambering or storm water drains or ditches and, if it has, it doesn't want to know. It wants to lay tarmac at however-many-million pounds a mile and move on.

This is a civilisation in decline. Even the business imperative has weakened and road haulage companies rely on the sturdiness of their foreign-made vehicles rather than the sturdiness of British roads to get goods quickly from A to B.

*

There is another way of looking at this kind of failure to do things which could be done and would benefit everyone. It is structural rather than historical. It starts from paradoxical observations such as this: Everyone uses pavements but, nonetheless, pavements are badly maintained. How come?

A small majority of citizens vote in British general elections but only a minority in local elections. You can win in local elections by getting just a few of your on-hand special interest groups to turn out for you. Pavement users are just not a special interest group and promising better pavements just isn't going to motivate a non-voter to go and vote. Nor is it going to switch a Tory or a Labour vote. It's nothing to get passionate about unlike whatever is the local passion evoker – the most common one, the threat of more house building. Local politicians support new house building at their peril.

Because there are no votes in pavements, there is no money for pavements. They have no advocates. They aren't slices of a cake you can fight over. That's the problem. Well-maintained pavements aren't the stuff of advocacy politics. No one group is going to get better off from better pavements. Everyone is. And no one is an advocate for everyone: read a batch of Opinion pieces in *The Guardian* – there are many – and they are about who should be getting a bigger slice of this or that cake, a bigger place in the sun. No one is going to pay you or encourage you to represent a common interest or even write opinion pieces about it. If one day better pavements arrive, everyone benefits regardless. No one has to contribute to get them.

Politicians - the professional political class with their own interests in shares of the cake - know that the route to power lies through assembling the voting support of enough sectional groups. In Britain, that mostly means people over sixty and what are always called ordinaryhardworking families - the sort of people temporarily encumbered with children but looking forward to the day when they too will be over sixty.

Pavements are not an issue but child care costs and pension benefits are. They are slices of the cake. Politicians make promises about these things, often engaging in competitive bidding. That could end up being costly, so sometimes they try a different strategy, appealing to sectional groups who won't be a burden on the Budget. It doesn't cost much to appeal to those wanting fox hunting bans (Labour) or gay marriages (Conservative). There's just the risk that you lose more votes than you gain.

But if you promise Better Pavements you are trying to appeal to everyone and Everyone is not a winning coalition. Pavements aren't adversarial enough, just painful when you trip over. Remember Winston Churchill: 1500 years without hot baths and central heating. Don't expect pavement improvements any time soon.

Further Reading:

Thomas Codrington, *The Maintenance of Macadamised Roads*. Second edition. E & F N Spon, London 1892.

Mancur Olson, *The Logic of Collective Action: Public Goods and the Theory of Groups*. Harvard University Press 1965

National identity

I just read Anne Frank's *Diary of a Young Girl* in the expanded 1990s edition published by Penguin Books:

> ...*my first wish after the war is to become a Dutch citizen. I love the Dutch, I love this country, I love the language and I want to work here. And even if I have to write to the Queen herself, I won't give up until I've reached my goal.*

Thus Anne Frank in her Diary entry for 11 April 1944. To say the least, it's an understandable wish for a displaced German Jew living in hiding in Amsterdam. Anne Frank listened to radio broadcasts by Queen Wilhelmina and members of the Dutch government exiled in London and took them very seriously. By going into exile, the Dutch leadership provided a focus of resistance to German occupation which could be heard and which helped Dutch people retain a sense of their identity and, equally, to identify themselves as resisters to foreign occupation. The Frank family in hiding was sustained by the support of four non-Jewish Dutch citizens.

Later in the Diary, Anne Frank is perturbed by signs of anti-semitism among the Dutch particularly aimed at German Jewish refugees (22 May 1944) and it was a Dutch citizen who finally betrayed the Franks' hiding place in August 1944. But even on 22 May she writes, *I love Holland. Once I hoped it would become a fatherland to me, since I had lost my own. And I hope so still!*

Citizenship - central to what we understand by National Identity - is normally acquired by accident of birth, just as it was originally for Anne Frank born in Frankfurt in 1929. It all depends on geography. At an extreme, national laws could make it the case that anyone born on national territory is automatically a citizen - even the child of a passing tourist who goes into premature labour in the wrong country. Countries move away from that extreme and lay down citizenship requirements - for example, that the child born on national territory needs to have one or both parents who are already nationals. Conversely, countries recognise as their own the child born in a foreign country to one of its nationals who has gone into labour there.

But as "birther" disputes about US presidential candidates show, the rules and feelings about what the rules should be can get very complicated, though geography remains central. Nine times out of ten (I guess) you get your first passport from the country where you were born. And your passport is not only what enables you to leave your country and get into another, it is - very traditionally - a guarantee of protection and a return ticket. Get into trouble in a foreign country and you can turn to your consulate. Get kicked out of a foreign country and however much they might wish not to let you and your obnoxious drunken stag party back in, your own country has to take you back, vomit and all. (It is really such bad publicity for my own country that I do wonder why the government doesn't ban stag parties from travelling abroad. They are a pathetic sight when you see them on the streets of some long-suffering European capital and they are not good company when you have to share a flight home with them). But to continue:

These banal facts about ordinary citizenship are worth thinking about partly because it was only in the period of Nazi domination in Europe that people found their citizenship routinely stripped from them (leaving them stateless and without protection) or found that their children could no longer benefit from the Geographical Principle. Zionism got its biggest boost from this aspect of Nazism. If geography will no longer secure you the ordinary protections of citizenship, then it is even more necessary to create a new country - Israel - where it is your race or religion or some mixture of them which will do the job instead. For a time, there were Zionists who felt that this could provide the basis for a working relationship with the Nazis: You don't want Jews in your country anymore? OK, then if you help us defeat the British in Palestine – provide weapons and so on - we will offer a home in Israel to as many Jews as you want to kick out from anywhere you like. It was as crude as that in the case of Avraham Stern of the Zionist paramilitary organisation known as the Lehi (the "Stern Gang" to the British occupiers). Hannah Arendt in her book *Eichmann in Jerusalem* (1963) fleshes out the details of attempts at rapprochement and accommodation between Zionists willing to mount attacks on the British occupiers in Palestine and the Nazis to whom they appealed.

Neither side – Nazi, Zionist – accepted the geographical principle as the basis of citizenship, but both had problems with their preferred alternatives. Trying to define "Jewishness" runs into the mirror-image of the problems the Nazis faced in trying to concoct some working definition of

"Aryan". Jewishness as a basis of citizenship has always been under pressure: on the one hand, there are today Arabs who hold Israeli citizenship in virtue of the geographical principle. On the other hand, there are Israelis who don't want to recognise the Jewishness of some of those knocking at the door - and who are, well, *different* or simply *black*.

Most right-wing nationalist movements aiming to raise the threshold for citizenship, to make sure you are Really One of Us, run into similar problems and fairly fast. An awful lot of people turn out to be Impure, including the nationalists themselves. This is also one of the main arguments in Shlomo Sand's *The Invention of the Jewish People* (2009) which says that in terms of blood, Palestinian peasant Muslims who are descended through many generations have a better claim to be Jewish by race than recently arrived and very mixed race self-identified Jewish settlers.

In more general terms, if you use a Blood Quantum to define belonging, it will either include people you don't intend to belong or exclude people you want on your side or both. In 1921 the US Congress passed the Hawaiian Homes Commission Act which reserved land in Hawai'i for native homesteaders. Anyone qualified as a native who was a descendant of not less than one-half part of the blood of the races inhabiting the Hawaiian Islands before 1778. That this was highly exclusionary is evident from the fact that at the time, the Hawaiian delegate to Congress (Hawai'i was not a State of the Union at this time), Prince Kalaniana'ole argued for a Blood Quantum of 1/32, a figure which can be understood in the context of inter-marriage and colonial rape and which also indirectly locates "belonging" at a cultural or even simply geographical level rather than at a racial level.

Purely geographical principles do have weaknesses and this is painfully clear in the case of my own country. Here, we all hold "United Kingdom" passports but there is not a single person who thinks that their identity is "United Kingdomish". Most of us when abroad will answer to being "British" (but not the Northern Irish who aren't) but when at home we are more likely to answer to being English, Welsh, Scots and Irish (with or, usually, without "Northern"). It depends on where we were born; where we live now and how long we have lived there; the football team we support (there is no United Kingdom football team though occasional attempts are made to get up a fake Potemkin-style team); our mother tongue which is sometimes Welsh and occasionally Scots or Irish Gaelic among hundreds of others; the language we speak now. And that's not an exhaustive list.

In the most recent 2011 United Kingdom census, Question 15 showed the confusion about identity with which we live. "How would you describe your national identity?" it asked, hopefully, inviting you to Tick all that apply:

[ ] English
[ ] Welsh
[ ] Scottish
[ ] Northern Irish
[ ] British
[ ] Other, write in

No one is going to write in "United Kingdomish". The United Kingdom is not a united nation. It may provide passports but it does not provide national identities. It only came into being a hundred years ago as a result of an Irish independence movement which only half achieved its aims. The London government sought to introduce Home Rule to all of Ireland but, at Protestant Irish gunpoint, was forced to hang on to six counties of the Irish colony Britain had created and tack them on to Great Britain.

The absence of a United Kingdom identity is sometimes painfully obvious. It doesn't have a National Anthem – in the dirge they are expected to sing, loyal subjects call on God to make the Queen feel good ("happy and glorious") and that's about it. If you don't believe in God or the Queen, you are a bit stuffed. No other principle of United Kingdom identity is on offer.

In the old days, when concert halls started the evening and cinemas ended with the National Anthem, I was one of those people who stayed seated. I recall an occasion when the concert-goer behind made valiant efforts to yank me to my feet. Another occasion was more interesting. There used to be a cinema in Oxford Street which showed European films and was popular with students. They screened *Ådalen 31* (Bo Widerberg, 1969), a powerful Swedish film about bad employers and good workers in the years before the social democratic party secured the hegemony which made Sweden a model for progressive politics - so much so, that I made Sweden the first foreign country I visited, in 1964 when I was seventeen. The audience was clearly moved by the film, but no sooner ended than the Anthem struck up. The juxtaposition was jarring and, without thinking, I shouted some protest. To my surprise, it was taken up and afterwards people gathered round to talk. More usually, in ordinary cinemas people simply walked out during the Anthem which is the real reason they gave up playing it. The Monarchy wasn't as popular then as our loyal press and

BBC now tirelessly works to make it. Nowadays, I stand up for the Anthem, not to embarrass those I am with. But in the sixties, we were all in it together.

On balance, I prefer weak principles of national identity like the Geographical Principle to strong ones like Blood and Race. But the United Kingdom is at an extreme end of a spectrum with only its Ruritanian monarchy to unite it. There is no national church, no national football team, a rubbish Eurovision entry, a rubbish Anthem, no common educational or legal system (since Scotland has its own). It is understandable that there are strong centrifugal elements and, now tipping the balance, I would welcome it if Scotland did decide to go it alone as a nation. It would force the issue in England and maybe enable England to shake off the dependencies of Wales and Northern Ireland. England does have a national anthem in Jerusalem, a national church (God help us), a football team, and a flag which is happily waved by every ethnic group. It has a fairly strong identity but one which is not the least based on Blood or Race though it is to some large extent on language.

*

What about Israel and Palestine? It may be that the best hope for peace is not a Two State solution based on strong principles of national identity, whether race or religion. It may be that the best hope is a one state solution with citizenship accorded on weak geographical principles but also open to those who love the country, love the languages and who want to work there and are willing to write to anyone who will listen to their case. It won't work very well for some of the same reasons that the United Kingdom doesn't work very well and, more importantly, because there is now a long history of mutual hatred constantly inflamed by religious extremists and foreign money. I don't know what to do about that; where the spirit of religion is very strong and diaspora money is poured into the pockets of those intent on domination, peace doesn't have much of a chance.

Ostentation

PRINCE Charles is a year younger than me. He has been heir to the throne for so long (since 1952 in fact) that if and when he becomes King and I am still alive, I shall continue to think of him as Prince Charles. Over the years I have watched his face age and the number of medals on his full dress uniforms increase. One day it occurred to me that most of his medals are birthday badges given to him by his Mum. He is still pinning them on sixty years after most of us stopped. They infantilise him.

In Africa during the past sixty years, kleptocratic and psychopathic tyrants, backed by their old colonial masters, have lorded it over impoverished peoples using a rhetoric of visual ostentation taken unashamedly from those former colonial rulers – and not just the British. But with no Mum to award them, they have simply had to award medals to themselves, getting some lackey to pin them on until their chests attain the full splendour of which Imperial kitsch is capable. The Emperor Bokassa - every whim indulged by the governments of France (Bokassa had uranium) - is the all-time outright winner for mirror-imaging the ostentation of the European Imperial powers. His coronation in 1976 cost the dirt-poor Central African Republic more than its entire annual state budget. The images are still worth Googling. You can see a copy of Ruritania's famous

Coronation coach and surrounding Bokassa, you can see *haute couture*-styled flunkeys like those – all male - who still surround Imperial President Hollande.

Bokassa's rivals have included General Idi Amin (with a taste for British military top-brass tassels) and Colonel Gadaffi (specialist in Italianate gold braid) and dozens of more forgettable bit players who have strutted and killed for a short while, all of them weighed down by this abject drive to outdo European levels of ostentation.

You might think it would shame Prince Charles into dressing a bit more like Nelson Mandela or maybe the Dalai Lama but, no, when it comes to keeping up appearances he is still determined to provide a role model for the next dictator up. One day, he hopes to live in a Palace where the Guards are dolled up in such a way that they could not guard a goldfish bowl and on hot days, no bare skin visible, collapse from heat exhaustion. It is both ostentation and irrationality. The tourists love it; it's much more fun than the Zoo.

In Charles's country, those who are likely to become his Subjects are introduced at an early age to irrational dress. The British not only do ostentatious uniform at the top; they do school uniform at the beginning. They really have a thing about it - some of it part of a long paedophilic tradition - and, if anything, it's getting worse. Parents off their heads on Janet and John think that education from three years up is about woollen caps and blazers and the more brightly be-ribboned the better for indicating your aspirations. Colour co-ordinated knee socks, striped ties, polished shoes, pleated skirts, boaters for summer, all obsessively listed in pages of Rules, declare that aspiration as a commitment to maintain Ruritania's social order and its established Table of Ranks.

British schools devote a great deal of time and money to devising and enforcing their uniform rules. It can be almost a full-time job for one Deputy Headteacher and they don't come cheap. Some parents grumble about the cost, forgetting that cost is partly what it's about – about showing that your child is in a different class to the riff-raff child in that school (unfortunately) just down the road. It is sometimes said that school uniform makes social distinctions less visible: you will not so easily spot the poor child in the classroom. But if you work back from the sharp-elbowed one-upmanship which characterises the uniforms of rival schools, it is most unlikely that social distinctions are not still visible in one school's classrooms. Showing yourself as better than someone else does not stop at the school gates.

British parents do not really find it possible to believe that there are successful countries, not plagued by juvenile delinquency or illiteracy, that manage to function *without any school uniform at all*. But dreadful as it may seem, they do exist, and if you want living proof of what can be done without the benefit of school uniform, check out the Cusanus-Gymnasium, Erkelenz, a German High School in a fairly ordinary town of just 45 000 people. It doesn't have a fancy website but you can get some idea there what the pupils look like. Normal is a word that comes to mind. Go to YouTube and – though I should give you a trigger warning that you will have to look at trai**rs - enjoy listening to the Erkelenz choir, the Oberstufenchor. They do English, of course. And lots more. Time and money isn't taken up with uniforms, you see. It's one reason German education gets better results.

Meanwhile, African dictators can still look to Prince Charles as a role model. British parents will take their cues from how the child known as Prince George is got up for school.

Passing for Female?

To my knowledge, no single or unified account of the limits and limitations of *self-identification* exists. Different practices prevail in different domains and reflect both fairly constant and sometimes rapidly changing perceptions of what is legitimate, what is safe, what is fair, and so on. The practices vary from one society to another, of course. The issue those practices address might be put like this: When can and should we accept someone's own word that they are *who* they say they are? When can and should we accept that they are *what* they say they are?

I began to think about identity and self-identification partly because of a well-publicised spat at Cardiff University. In 2015, Germaine Greer, writer and celebrity, author of *The Female Eunuch* and other works, was invited to lecture at Cardiff. It nearly didn't happen because the women's officer of the Student Union there, Rachael Melhuish, got up a petition to No Platform her:

> *Greer has demonstrated time and time again her misogynistic views towards trans women, including continually misgendering transwomen and denying the existence of transphobia altogether. Trans-exclusionary views should have no place in feminism or society.*

As an example of her "transphobia", Greer was notably called out for the use of the expression "ghastly parodies" to describe those whose birth sex was Male but who subsequently choose to present in society as women, either with or without surgery. Greer refuses to accept the self-presentation or, at least, some of those presentations. In contrast, Melhuish aligns herself with those who think that people should be allowed to self-identify their gender and be treated accordingly. That is in line with the policy of the National Union of Students. How plausible is that position? It seems to me that it helps if we consider the argument in the context of other cases where identity questions arise.

Banks no longer accept that you are who you say you are or that you live where you say you live. You have to provide proof in both cases – and the banks spell out to you what kind of proof they will accept (your passport, a recent utility bill, and so on). This is justified as an anti-fraud / anti-money laundering / anti-tax evasion measure. We are not supposed to get indignant when asked to prove that we are who we say we are, though I imagine that there was a time when people (especially those in higher social classes) would indeed have become indignant: "How dare you!"

Compare situations in which you are simply asked to declare something and that's it. When you go into hospital you are asked to declare your religion and they just write down what you say. This will affect how your body will be handled if you die there and who will seek to visit you if you are dying. And so on. You declare and no one queries it. Thus it is that in the United Kingdom there are very many more self-declared Christians than enter Christian churches. The self-ascription "Christian" on a hospital form is for all practical purposes a negative characterisation: Well, I'm certainly not a Jew or a Muslim and I don't want to answer "None" just in case …

But in other contexts, this casual attitude to religious self-ascription would not be tolerated. In England, school admissions provide a good example. Since the 1990s, successive governments have encouraged a greater degree of social segregation through the mechanism of "Faith Schools" which are allowed to select their pupils by the religious affiliation of their parents. However, realising that parents are only too willing to perjure themselves to get their kids into nice middle class schools, our more popular faith schools now look for proof that you are indeed of the religious persuasion that you claim. They impose religious tests. Indignation? Not at all. Our modern parents (sociologists tell us) are more than happy to present themselves in the pews of the local Church of England or Roman Catholic church where for as long as it takes they sit smugly, ghastly parodies of religious belief.

In the UK, there are few contexts in which self-identification by race or ethnicity is asked for other than for statistical purposes – the Census, notably. We don't have Quotas and we don't have Exclusions. In some contexts, notably medical, the accuracy of self-identification is important: there are some genetic disorders and diseases which discriminate by race and it can be important for a doctor to know whether or not you are in a high risk group. In this case, people have a self-interest in making accurate self-identifications.

But in other societies, self-identification by race or ethnicity or their official ascription have long and complex histories and important consequences. Everyone is familiar with the idea of "Passing for White" which in the United

93

States was – and maybe still is – a rational strategy for improving your life chances. If your skin is pale enough, then that opens up the possibility of passing for white and, if you decide to do that even in the knowledge that your ancestry is at least partly non-white, then you acquire immediate social advantages - but at the same time usually have to live with inner conflict and the anxiety that you may be found out. On the other side from "Passing for White", when forms of positive discrimination are introduced designed to favour disadvantaged groups then there are also possibilities of abuse and once again Tests have to be introduced to verify that you are who you say you are or what you say you are. It is not unknown for people to choose to "Pass for Black".

But most of the time in daily life, people don't encounter many occasions when their self-identifications are challenged. Being asked for your age ID when trying to enter a club or pub is as bad as it gets and that problem, unfortunately, goes away naturally.

*

Now let's go back to the Melhuish – Greer conflict. I have always understood that a man who dresses as a woman is correctly described as a transvestite and that a man who in addition has undergone hormonal treatment or surgery is usually described as a transsexual. More or less the same categorisation can be made in relation to women who present themselves as men. Neither category tells us anything about a trans person's sexual orientation. Nor does it actually tell us much about their gender since it is not spelled out what it is to present oneself as a woman (or when the transition is made in the other direction, a man). The National Union of Students wants us to treat the presentation of self as unproblematic ("My Identity Is Not Your Business", Resolution 106, December 2015) whereas I thought that a great deal of social theory and most feminisms from Simone de Beauvoir (at the latest) onwards were about it being extremely problematic.

Does it mean in the M to F case presenting oneself according to the local gender stereotypes of what it is to be a woman? Does it mean presenting oneself as a woman in one's dress and the public toilets you enter? Does it mean signalling to men that they should treat you (according to the conventions in place) as a woman? And likewise, signalling the same to women – so that, for example, you can claim admission to "Women Only" meetings? Does it mean signalling to others that you feel more comfortable presenting yourself and being treated as a woman (whatever that happens to mean), pretty much regardless of how you dress, what toilets you use, what personality traits you display, and so on?

The basis of a 2015 film, David Ebershoff's novel *The Danish Girl*, originally published in 2000, offers - perhaps unwittingly - answers to some of these questions. It does not stay close to the true story which inspired it, but nonetheless it allows us to see what some of the real-world issues are. A large part of the narrative is about a man, Einar, passing as a woman, Lili, in various ways, some of them morally dubious: for example, when through your dress, you misrepresent your sexual identity to someone you want to seduce or be seduced by. Whereas feminism since the 1960s has most often been about challenging conventional gendering, urging women to be more assertive and men less macho, women to be less obsessed with their appearance and men less demanding in that regard, Eberhsoff's transgender character embraces wholly conventional gendering but simply switches sides. That appears to be the case for some contemporary real-life switchers: they accept the existing conventions on both sides, but switch allegiances.

Passing as a woman normally involves more than asking to be labelled a certain way. The exceptions are provided, notably, by cases – largely in the past - where birth-sex women cross-dressed as men in order to gain admission to armies, medical schools, and so on, but who did not in any way feel that they were something other than women. There were also cases where men cross-dressed as women, usually for nefarious purposes like escaping military service or gaining access to places where young females could be found who might be available for heterosexual sex.

But the most obvious cases of cross-dressing occurred (and still occur) on stage where the Pantomime Dame or the burlesque Drag Queen have for a very long time (centuries?) presented a comedy of "ghastly parodies" . Sometimes these parodies appear off stage and may have been in Germaine Greer's mind. Would the defenders of trans people's rights welcome a Pantomime Dame to a Women Only meeting?

That sort of question may be a way into thinking about the whole issue. If you would not admit a Pantomime Dame, my guess is that is because you think they are simply a man pretending to be a woman. Fine, it's not really in dispute. Next question: How about an old-fashioned male - to-female transvestite who cuts a very striking figure in high heels and booming voice? Is that person more than a

Pantomime Dame, but just off-stage? If so, what makes the difference? What has to happen to qualify that person for a "Women Only" meeting? Do they just have to Pass in the way that the Dame and the old fashioned transvestite Fail, namely, the ability to Pass? And who is to make up the rules and judge who Passes?

Germaine Greer has said that "just because you lop off your dick it doesn't make you a woman". This is obviously true: men have their dicks lopped off in car crashes, industrial accidents and - most frequently - misadventures with military high explosives. Few of them breathe a sigh of relief or think "Now I can be the woman I always wanted to be". Greer is saying that even if you lose your dick as part of a self-mutilation or voluntarily undergone medical procedure, that in itself is not *sufficient* to make you a woman, not enough to get you into the "Women Only" meeting. That seems correct: you need a supporting story which explains why you did it and how it forms part of the "woman" identity you are claiming. It seems to me quite possible that someone whose dick is intact could have a stronger claim than a dickless person to be regarded as a woman.

Rachael Melhuish is right in this: people who are gratu-itously offensive to others generally deserve a put-down of some kind if we can be reasonably clear what we mean by "gratuitously offensive". Greer has always been foul mouthed and blunt and that is one reason she achieved iconic status as a feminist. If she thinks an argument is ridiculous, she will say so and that does not always go down well. It's not obviously the same thing as being gratuitously offensive. It is not offensive to shred a bad argument; it is one of the things students are supposed to do.

*

Freudian psychoanalysis is hated only and always by those who insist that we are always who we say we are and what we say we are. I am a kind and loving person, always – and if you dispute those Facts, I will cast you into outer darkness.

But most aspects of our selves are not things we can will, and those who believe that the will can always triumph are doomed to failure. My will won't triumph over my tooth-ache and I can't will away primary sexual characteristics or even many of the secondary gender characteristics I have acquired. Several critics of the NUS's recent positions use the word "fascist" or allude to it (as I have done in referencing Leni Riefenstahl's 1935 film *Triumph of the Will*) in describing its politics. I think this is because of a suspicion that there is a background belief here that all of life is about resolutions, decisions and will-power. Take away the reference to Fascism and an alternative might be to call such beliefs *The Anorexic Mistake*. They are beliefs which cluster around the idea that we can subject our bodies and our selves entirely to control by our will power.

I realise that earlier I used examples – the Pantomine Dame, the Drag Queen - which may seem trivial, though that's a familiar device to clarify complex issues and it sometimes works. But in reality, from what I read, trans people have much more difficult lives than the Pantomime Dame, as do Hermaphrodites - Intersex persons - who start from a different anatomical situation.

It is hard and often enough anguishing to realise that you are only going to feel more authentic, more comfortable, more desirable if you shift into a mode of self-presentation which asks other people to reclassify your gender, more or less regardless of the state of your sexual organs. But just because it's hard does not mean that a Narrative of Suffering or a Hard Luck story on its own should open the doors to the Women Only meeting. The narrative needs to be convincing and the story true. In the UK, a 2004 Act of Parliament attempted to deal with the matter by creating a Gender Recognition Panel. It may be that the legislation will need to be modified but it seems to me unlikely we will conclude that so little is at stake that anyone can self-declare who and what they are for all purposes. Those who appear to want simple self-declaration to suffice are arguing for something which can place others at risk of harm – it has occasionally happened already that males with heterosexual interests and a tendency to violence declare themselves women to gain access to Women Only spaces.

So the stories we tell cannot always let us off the hook of other forms of accountability. Likewise, just because you may encounter hostile or dismissive reactions does not mean that you are automatically to be reckoned morally superior to those around you. You will still have your own weaknesses and unkindnesses – things which make every-one uncomfortable with themself at one time or another, things which we would like to wish away with a "No, that's not me". We can never be entirely who we say we are or what we say we are. That's just one of life's unfairnesses. But at least it applies to everyone.

*

At the back of my mind I have this thought. The history of medicine is littered with histories of doctors doing terrible things to people, supposedly to "cure" them of this or that.

Some of the medical techniques employed to re-configure sexual characteristics have been around a long time: sheikhs had eunuchs in their harems, the Vatican had castrati in its choirs (until 1913 or 1959, sources differ on the dates), German sex clinics began offering operations in the 1920s, chemical castration was around in the 1950s to punish homosexuals like Alan Turing, the major industry which services the desire for larger breasts is very well established. The range of surgeries and chemistries available continues to grow. But there is a possibility that a hundred years from now, those who by then believe themselves to be progressive and humane may regard at least some of those techniques as barbaric - even when self-chosen - and as falsely offering cures for catastrophic dilemmas which require other modes of approach.

Even now, when I read up on the history of Lili Elbe [Lili Elvenes] (1882 -1931), the so-called *Danish Girl*, I find myself uneasy when I discover that her fourth and final surgery, submitted to when she was 49 years old, killed her. It was carried out in Dresden and involved the unprecedented transplant of either ovaries or a uterus. It reads just too much like an irresponsible medical experiment conducted on a vulnerable person who was past normal child bearing age. Worse, it occurs in a political context where medical irresponsibility was soon to achieve political sanction and encouragement. Dr Warnekros who operated on Lili in 1931 joined the Nazi party in 1933. Put into that kind of context, sex change operations at that time belong to the same world as medical experimentation on those who had not consented, to forced sterilisation and other eugenic policies which culminated in the mass killing of the mentally feeble and physically handicapped.

Questionable Narratives

My mother was born in 1907, the youngest of seven children. Her mother (Eliza Stevens née Turner) was forty at the time and her father (Thomas Redsell Stevens) a few years older. As a boy, he had run away from home to join the Navy. Somewhere I have a medal from the Battle of the Nile in the 1880s. After that, he joined a Crayford armaments firm, Vickers, and worked outdoors as a gun tester - a job in which he lost an arm. The family lived in Sutton at Hone, a Kent village, in a Victorian terrace house a short walk from The Butts where the guns were tested. My mother left school at fourteen (or, more likely, thirteen) and went to work in the local paper mill.

I was born in 1947 and grew up with a long view of history. When my mother spoke about The War she quite often meant the First. I must be one of the few people alive able to sing the song which she and other children sang as they skipped behind German Prisoners of War being marched to a camp near her home:

> *At the Cross, At the Cross*
> *Where the Kaiser lost his Horse*
> *And the Eagle on his hat flew away*
> *He was eating German buns*
> *When he heard the British Guns*
> *And the artful little bugger ran away*

There were aspects of my upbringing that linked me to an even older past. As a child, I was urged to eat the bitter lettuce on my plate with the words "It's got lodnum in it". Lodnum, in case you haven't worked it out, is laudanum which is Good for You. It's the kind of thing which now makes me think that I grew up acquiring negative cultural capital.

My mother talked family history to me from as early in my life as I can remember and she included her own explanations of family dynamics. Her father – he died twenty years before I was born - had a fiery temper, she told me, and this was owing to the fact that his mother was Irish (maiden name Redsell) and, as was then known, the Irish have fiery tempers.

My father also had a temper but this was combined with a domineering manner, and these she attributed to the fact that his own father (my Grandfather Pateman) came from a German family. My father did not help matters by sporting a moustache. My father was also very mean, a fact I learnt early in life, and my mother attributed this to the fact that his own mother was clearly Jewish - you had only to look at her nose.

These national and racial stereotypes were mobilised without any malice. Indeed, my mother took her Bible seriously and believed that we are all equal before God. On this basis, when women in saris began to appear in our local streets, she made a point of saying *Good Morning* to each of them as she made her way to the shops. She told me that they must feel very lonely being in a strange country and this was her way of making them feel welcome.

When I was a teenager and began to put two and two together, I realised that the family history my mother had narrated made me, in some proportion, a German Irish Jew. I quite liked this exotic thought and treasured it for many years. Unfortunately, it's not true. When much later in life I did my Internet Genealogy, tracking back to c. 1800 the histories of the thirty dead people who immediately precede me (two parents, four grandparents, eight ...), I found not one of them born outside southern England and all of them leading the lives of labourers and skilled artisans or the children and spouses thereof.

My mother's grandmother Redsell may have been of Irish descent but when I research the family, it is in Crayford Kent as far back as I can go (circa 1800). My paternal grandfather has a surname which occurs (as Patemann) in Germany and the facial look is plausible - but he was a London Pateman and they originated from farm labourers who left the Midlands or East Anglia for the city. My London- born paternal grandmother had a very un-English look and her maiden name (Veryard) is sometimes claimed to be of French Huguenot origin and her family came from a part of the country (Castle Cary in Somerset) linked to Huguenot Veryards. So it seems I'm not a bit of a Jew and probably not even a bit of a Huguenot because that connection may be some Internet wishful thinking. It's a bit of a disappointment. But, it's true, my grandmother did have a very big nose.

My mother never linked her own mother to a national or racial stereotype, not even an English one. She always linked her to a gender stereotype. Her mother was the Angel in the House, a model of patience and devotion who could do no wrong. After the death of her father in 1925 when she was 18, my mother gradually became the new Angel in the House, living at home (the youngest daughter) and looking after her own mother as her health declined. When my parents married in 1938, my father moved into the household. In that period before the war, my mother gave birth at full-term to a still-born child (a girl who would have been called Elizabeth) and in the distress which followed, cut her own throat. But she stabbed in the middle rather than cutting at the side. This fact I know because when I was 11 or 12, my father shouted it out to me as a vicious aside in the middle of one of many tirades directed against his wife. My mother later told me that what he had shouted was true, adding that she thought of my birth a decade later as God's Forgiveness. Unto us a son is given. Not the easiest narrative to carry around. My mother set me on a life-long course of thinking about Women's Problems. In contrast, Men's Problems remain to me a largely unknown country.

Respect as Political Correctness

More often than I would like, I read some new story of something condemned as "political correctness gone mad" and I sometimes find myself in agreement with the critics. I find myself suspicious of the people who get up campaigns to ban this or that and unimpressed with the arguments they advance. At the heart of my unease is a sense that we are often enough in thrall to people who, given half a chance, would love to be working as full-time bureaucrats in some police organisation for the promotion of virtue and suppression of vice. And very unpleasant bureaucrats they would be. It's likely to be the case, of course, that some are indeed already working for the police as undercover officers just like those previously deployed under successive British governments to discredit environmental campaigners. But leave that thought aside.

It's not so long ago that England did have a government department for the promotion of virtue and suppression of vice. Until 1968, if you wanted to present a new play on a public stage, you required the prior approval of the Lord Chamberlain's Office, an official body within the Ruritanian Royal Household dating back to 1737. In the end, people (especially playwrights and theatre managers) tired of the ludicrous changes demanded by this anachronistic bureaucracy and even more tired of the outright bans.

Eventually, it was abolished by Parliament and very few people had any regrets. Those who did took the opportunity to sponsor a "family values" theatre where you could go safe in the knowledge that you would not be amused, shocked or provoked. I never went there but I did go to see the first new London stage play to open after the ending of censorship, the musical *Hair*. And, yes, at the end I did dance on stage.

The Lord Chamberlain's office had no clear sense of what it was that it wanted to discourage. Immorality. Things which would not be suitable for a Sunday School perform-ance. Potential *double entendres*. It was really no more than a dusty catalogue of prejudices and insecurity and plain stupidity which guided them. This is how Britain's leading theatre director, Peter Hall, recalled the Office, writing about it in 2002:

> *The Lord Chamberlain's office was largely staffed by retired naval officers with extraordinarily filthy minds. They were so alert to filth that they often found it when none was intended. I remember calling on their office to plead for the reinstatement of some lines that had been inexplicably cut from a play I was directing. "We all know what's going on here, Hall, don't we?" said the retired naval officer angrily. "It's up periscopes." "Up periscopes?" I queried. "Bug-gery, Hall, buggery!" Actually, it wasn't.*

It was often as ludicrous as that, and not just in the Lord Chamberlain's office. Remember that when Penguin Books was prosecuted for publishing D H Lawrence's *Lady Chatterley's Lover* in 1960, the prosecuting counsel Mervyn

Griffith-Jones addressing the Jury really did ask them if they felt the book was one "you would wish your wife or servants to read" - a question for which he will be ridiculed until the end of time. Unless, of course, opinion changes and we decide that in England, Saudi Arabia should be our role model. They still know how to do wives and servants. We supply them with massive amounts of military hardware to help keep it that way.

But if "political correctness gone mad" is to be feared, is there still a sane version of political correctness which should be supported? Yes, very definitely so. But what does the sane version look like? How can it be articulated so as to see off the witch hunters? How can it be formulated so that we know how to operate it with a high degree of consensus?

At the heart of public policy as it has developed in England over my lifetime is the idea that a civilised society and a democratic society can only be sustained if and when people routinely grant *respect* to all those they encounter in daily life, including in their life as public officials. Most of our encounters are with people we know little about beyond their appearance, how they look and how they sound. And we absolutely should not use how they look or how they sound to calibrate the degree of respect (or disrespect) which we accord them. You just cannot use the colour of a person's skin, the sex or gender they present to you, their accent, their dress, their presumed social class or educational level, their religious beliefs if those can be inferred … you cannot use any of those to calibrate how and whether you say "Please", "Thank you", "Excuse me", and so on. That is basic *respect*, that is basic *civility*. The look or the sound of someone gives you absolutely no basis for withholding or graduating civility. By extension, accidental characteristics are not a legitimate basis for deciding who gets to be interviewed for jobs, offered jobs or housing, prioritised for medical treatment or favoured for jail sentences.

Back in 1973, I sat through the trial in Exeter of Dr Rose Dugdale an upper-class English heiress who was accused of stealing the family silver in a midnight raid on her parents' home. I was her lay legal adviser (her McKenzie Friend as it was then known). Rose Dugdale was a feisty woman, to use an expression probably not in use then. But in Exeter, Mr Justice Park looked at Dugdale and looked at her partner and co-accused, working-class Walter Heaton, and decided – as he told the Court – that She was under the influence of He - an argument Dugdale had never used in her defence and which must have seemed ludicrously untrue to anyone who had observed the trial, in which she defended herself. Nonetheless, He got banged up in Parkhurst for quite a stretch and She got a suspended sentence - free to go off to Ireland, hijack a helicopter, drop bombs on a police station and carry out what at the time was the world's largest art theft. Well, then she did get banged up but she had to try a lot harder than Walter Heaton. Discrimination always has unintended consequences. If Mr Justice Park had not deployed female vulnerability - still with us in the cliché *vulnerableyoungwomen* - to deny Rose Dugdale her prison sentence, the course of Irish history may well have been different.

Respectful behaviour towards someone is also inherently politically correct behaviour since society as a whole has an interest (self-interest) in sustaining polite, respectful and civilised face to face conduct. I have made that sound a bit old-fashioned. Never mind, it is really quite radical: it is the kind of thought which makes it difficult for someone like Jeremy Corbyn to kneel when he meets the Queen because it is the other end of a spectrum of behaviour which delivers only a grunt to a woman at a supermarket till. For the same reason, a public official doing their job properly will say to the person trying to pull rank, "No, you will have to wait your turn like everyone else". That is politically correct - and quite right too.

Starting from the core value of respect, it will be immediately clear in some cases what should not be tolerated. When people are discriminated against for employment or housing or education on the same irrelevant grounds as lead to failures of respect, then society as a whole has an interest in intervening to discourage it, prohibit it and, in serious cases, punish it when it does occur. Discrimination always weakens a society, creating real injustice and a sense of injustice but also, very simply, making it less sustainable. But in many cases, it will not be so clear what should not be tolerated. And in those cases, rather than proceeding stridently – which is one of the problems we have at present – we should proceed with care. Because it's not blindingly obvious what is right and what is wrong. It requires thoughtful debate to decide what to do in a difficult case.

A good example is provided by the Bake Me a Cake dispute, a case where one of the important players changed his mind. The story is this: in 2014 a Christian-run Belfast bakers was asked by a gay rights activist to bake a cake decorated with the words "Support Gay Marriage". The bakers refused – on the grounds that the slogan was contrary to their Christian beliefs - and the activist, with support from a publicly-funded Equality organisation, took them to court and the court found in his favour, upholding a claim of unlawful discrimination. At this stage, the case was supported by Peter Tatchell, probably the best known UK gay rights activist. The case went to appeal but just before that appeal, Tatchell wrote an article for *The Guardian* saying that he had changed his mind. It was never claimed that the bakery would have discriminated against the customer just because he was gay – refusing his custom even if he wanted no more than to buy a jam doughnut – just that the bakery refused to make his message. Tatchell says that the laws invoked in the case were never intended to make people promote political ideas with which they disagreed and writes, "Discrimination against people should be unlawful, but not against ideas". All this is argued in a sober fashion and makes an important distinction which is certainly worth thinking about, at the very least.

I don't think the issue is completely clear cut. The bakers weren't asked to support gay marriage but asked to use their professional skills to assist someone else who wanted to support it. Small printers do this all the time, printing leaflets for political parties they don't support and may well loathe. Of course, small printers probably feel that they have a right to draw the line somewhere, willing to print for nearly everyone but not That Lot whoever That Lot may be. In those circumstances, That Lot would probably take their custom elsewhere and not think that it was a matter for some court of law. It is indeed chilling that a spat over a cake decoration can go to court [See Endnote]. The Christian bakers just happened to draw their line in a place which put them up against another powerful branch of local conservatism. I can't see a bunch of local anarchists taking bakers to court for refusing a slogan, though they might spray it on the shop window as revenge.

Tatchell's willingness to take a fresh look at the case, change his mind and come up with a conclusion which is not self-interested will have angered some people and nowadays it is predictable that will produce a hostile response and it did. Fortunately, Tatchell – a very brave man - is hardened to abuse. But it is still disturbing that not only Twitter but universities too are now full of people who don't know how to argue or who don't have an argument and can only do shock, anger, name-calling, trolling, and demands for apology (preferably grovelling). Some of these people are bullies, some probably don't realise that they don't know how to argue a case, some are disturbed, some are very good at acting up their offence. All quickly take up absolutist positions: No Debate, No Platform, Fuck Off and Die. Nowadays you can go a long way in student politics on that Manifesto. But circling the wagons is not political correctness. The latter's overarching aim is to unify, not divide; to include wherever possible. Its Utopia is a society in which everyone at the very least is willing to be civil to everyone else, not a society where you are the last person left standing at the microphone.

Endnote:

A lot of my unease in this case and in others relates to the use of regular courts. I don't like courts and I don't think they are fit for some of the things they are now expected to deal with. Some of the disputes which end up in court would be better dealt with through mediation, truth and reconciliation, face to face confrontation, financial compensation or, in some cases, simply doing nothing. Courts do not bring about change. A court will not alter the views of Christian bakers, and the satisfaction of a winner is merely the satisfaction of a pound of flesh. Courts sharpen conflicts into polarised form, you are either Guilty or Not Guilty and quite often it's not that simple. Whatever rough justice courts do dispense is sometimes totally unbalanced by the outlet they provide for the madness of newspapers and the crowds they incite.

Social Mobility

Home

In 1961 my mother left my father – really, was driven out – subsequently gaining a legal separation on grounds of mental cruelty and neglect to maintain; I don't know if such categories are still used. In 1962, after lodging with my mother's brother and his wife for a year, my mother (then aged fifty-four) and I (fourteen) moved to 16 Sheridan Road, Lower Belvedere administratively in Kent but really in south east London, close to Plumstead and Woolwich.

I will describe the accommodation in detail.

The flat occupied the ground floor of a Victorian red-brick terraced house, divided into two with a shared front door and hallway and stairs leading to the upstairs flat, occupied by a London docker and his wife, Mr and Mrs Gerrard.

The first room off the hall was quite spacious with west-facing double sash windows, making it light. This was my mother's bedroom and remained so until she died in 1978. It had no heating - there was no electric socket. For some time, it was without floor covering, but my mother had a dressing table and wardrobe. At some point, we were given a large carpet (bloodstained, which is why we were given it) and I think my mother later added an armchair so that she could sit in the room on sunny days.

The next room off the hall was my room until I went to University in 1965; I used it in vacations and later intermittently. It also had no heating, again because there was no electric socket, though there was an old gas lamp still supplied with gas. I lit it on a couple of occasions but did not dare risk regular use. There was no floor covering. There were large windows facing east and in winter this room was very cold with ice sometimes forming on the inside of the window panes. I had a wardrobe and built-in cupboard.

I studied for my A levels in this room, sitting on a stool and using the top of a chest of drawers as my desk, and if it was cold, I wore my overcoat. In this room I memorised large parts of Samuelson - my A level textbook of economics.

The third door in the hallway led to the living room, a small damp room with a small window looking into the back yard. There was an electric socket allowing this room to be heated and to house a wireless. It was on this valve wireless that I heard the news of President Kennedy's assassination. I recall this as the last time that I consciously prayed. I continued through my teens to be interested in religion but ceased to believe. My mother read her Bible regularly and when modern translations of the Bible appeared (the New English Bible), I gave them to her as birthday presents.

My mother's brothers and sisters gave us a dining table and two upright chairs, two armchairs, a sideboard, and a china display cabinet. To begin with, we had newspaper on the living room floor to stop the draughts through the boards and later we were given some lino. It was after I had gone to University that my mother acquired a television. She never acquired a telephone, but there was a public booth opposite the house and, in time, she learnt to use this. But when at eighteen I collapsed with an allergic reaction to the antibiotics prescribed to me for bronchitis, she fetched the doctor by running to his surgery.

A cupboard off this room was the pantry and in warm weather a bucket of cold water was placed inside to help keep milk cool.

A door off the living room led to the kitchen, which I painted and tiled soon after we moved in. There was a deep sink with a cold tap, a gas cooker, and a copper which used gas to heat water either for boiling clothes or for supplying hot water to the tin bath kept in a corner. I had a bath once a week. This organisation of the kitchen did not change in the sixteen years my mother lived in the flat.

Outside, there was a pair of brick-built toilets, one for each of the two flats. As there was no light, after dark you took a torch.

In 1963, the Headmaster of Marlborough College, John Dancy, published a book *The Public Schools and the Future* which I read. As you do when you are an angry young teenager, I wrote to him expressing my scepticism and in reply received an invitation to stay at Marlborough for a few days, accompanied by a few of my fellow Bromley Grammar School sixth formers. In exchange, we were expected to accept a return visit and a boy called Charles Hicks lodged with me - he had my bed and I slept on the floor. I think my home must have been a talking point, because another Marlborough boy, Redmond O'Hanlon, asked to swap with Hicks. My mother said no.

The rent was about thirty shillings (£1.50) per week and my

mother had a basic income of about £5 per week. Because my father did not pay his court-ordered maintenance, and because my mother was much of the time not fit enough to work, we were supported by the National Assistance Board (later the Ministry of Social Security). In addition to their support, from the age of 15 I received allowances from Kent County Council for school uniform and a Free Dinner pass. I also worked in my school holidays, beginning when I reached my 15th birthday in July 1962 and took a summer holiday job with the London Trustee Savings Bank in Fleet Street. I forget how much I earned though the figure of £3-something comes to mind, about half of which went on train fares.

Bromley Grammar School for Boys   1958 - 1964

Sociologists distinguish between Contest and Sponsored social mobility. Contests are things like Civil Service Examinations - if you pass you move to the next stage; if you don't, you don't - even if your father is a very important person. Sponsorship is usually equated with nepotism, but it also includes talent spotting of various kinds. Some people only become upwardly mobile because they are picked out, encouraged, flattered or coerced.

From 1958 to 1964 I attended Bromley Grammar School for Boys in Kent. I had passed the 11+ and this is the Grammar School my parents picked for me. Or, rather, my mother picked: she had heard boys from the local grammar school (Dartford) swearing in the street; so I was sent to a town fifteen miles away with whose streets she was unfamiliar. Neither of my parents, none of my aunts and uncles, had attended such a school and they were all early school leavers.

I was in the top stream, though between 1958 and 1961 my class position deteriorated as things got worse at home. After my mother and I left, it began to improve. Top stream boys sat four 'O' levels (English, Latin, French, Maths) in the fourth form and, if they passed all of them, could skip the fifth year (and all Science 'O' levels!) and go straight into the Sixth Form as I did in Autumn of 1962, just after my 15th birthday.

By this time, I was a member of the Awkward Squad of difficult pupils, argumentative and out of line - school uniform and such like. I wanted to take 'A' levels in Economics, French and Maths. "Sticky" Richardson who had taught me Maths declined to have me in his sixth form group, so did Mr May, the French teacher. The Economics master, the charismatic Alan Charnley, had not encountered me so I got into his group. "Jack" Addison took me for History and I was also accepted for Geography by another master who hadn't previously taught me (Mr Moffatt, who was very good). You had to sign up for General Studies (Mr Atkins) and a further 'O' level - I chose Italian. In my own time, I did a voluntary 'O' level in Art - Awkward Squad members found the atmosphere in the Art room therapeutic.

Early on in my sixth form studies, the Deputy Head took me aside and told me that I would not be made a Prefect. Too rebellious. Curiously, the same man ("Polly" Parrott) also got me to deputise for him when he could not teach our Italian class - I had a good accent and could give dictation.

More importantly, I was also told I had been selected for the Oxbridge Scholarship group. At Bromley GS, you did not put yourself forward for Oxbridge. They selected you for the group which would stay on for an extra term after taking 'A' levels and prepare for the Scholarship exams. Not only that, they told you which University, which college and which degree. In my case, Oxford, St Peter's and PPE - exactly the same combination as for my school friend John Edward King - now an Economics Professor in Australia -who was accelerated even faster and went to Oxford at 16 or 17 and had an Oxford extra-mural lectureship by the age of 20. In the meantime, those in the Oxbridge group would also be pushed in various ways.

In the mornings, as we entered school, the Headmaster "Henry" Anderson would stand outside his study and observe us. Boys were called over for various reasons. On one occasion, he spotted my Chelsea boots and dressed me down. On another, he called me in to tell me that my father (who I had refused further contact with when I reached the age of 16) had been to the school and had left some papers for me to sign: my father had bought National Savings Bonds in my name and now required me to sign them over to him.

On several occasions, the Head called me over to say he had something on his desk that he thought I should read. They were actually Government reports. As a sixth former I read the Beeching report on the future of the railways and the Robbins report on the future of higher education. And I read them cover to cover. This is how you were informally prepared for the Oxbridge scholarship examinations.

My Economics teacher, Alan Charnley, also took an interest in me and wanted the school to put me up for Christ Church or some such, but he was over-ruled. The school's strategy was to maximise the number of names on the Oxbridge Scholarship board - which hung in the main entrance hall – and putting me up for the same degree course at St Peter's the year after John Edward King probably seemed a racing certainty. When I got my A level results,

Charnley also suggested that I write and ask to be interviewed at St Peter's before the Scholarship exam, which I did. They gave me a place but told me to sit the exam anyway - and, indeed, out of it I got an Open Scholarship which in those days was worth £60 on top of your grant which in my case was a full grant of £370, so the scholarship was worth having. My mother's income at the time was about £250 per year.

Without my school's sponsorship, I would not have applied to Oxford. There were a couple of boys whose middle-class parents intervened when they were not put into the Oxbridge group but mine would never have done so. And despite being a member of the Awkward Squad, I don't think I would have pushed myself forward. I did want to go to University and I had fall-back choices - the new universities - if I did not get into Oxford.

Of course, this little story of Sponsored Mobility also reveals one of its weaknesses. If my teachers had been just a little bit spiteful, they could have punished me for all the trouble I caused them by keeping my name off that Oxbridge list. Fortunately for me, they were above such meanness.

St Peter's College, Oxford   1965 – 1968

Though I have always believed that my school picked St Peter's for me on the grounds that it was easier to get into than one of the colleges basically reserved for boys from top public schools, my school probably did not know that St Peter's also had some commitment to "widening access", though perhaps not in the sense we now understand it.

St Peter's Hall was founded as a Private Hall in 1929

*to commemorate the life and teaching of the Right
Reverend Frances James Chavasse ...formerly Lord
Bishop of Liverpool ...with the object ... (a) To
maintain and promote education, religion and learning for and among students generally of whatever
religious persuasion and especially to give aid to
students in straitened or reduced circumstances ...*

This from the college statutes. In practice, Pot Hall (as it
was known even after it became a full college of the
University in 1961) provided university places for the sons
- it was single sex - of Church of England clergymen,
especially those of an evangelical persuasion and lacking
the private means to send their boys to top public schools
and thence to top Oxbridge colleges.

When I arrived in 1965 the sons of the clergy were still
there in large numbers and it rather depressed me to
discover how modest were their academic achievements -
Ds and Es at "A" level whereas I had three shiny grade As.
The college had an abysmal ranking in the university tables
which were produced by scoring the degree results students
achieved.

I discovered that it was an expectation attached to my
£60 Scholarship that I should read lessons at services in the
College chapel and lead grace at the beginning of meals
[Benedictus, Benedicat ...] and one of the first things I had
to do on arrival was excuse myself by writing to the Master
of the College, Canon Julian Percy Thornton-Duesbery, an
Evangelical and prominent Moral Re-Armer. He was also
a supervisor of the right-wing, evangelical Oxford Inter-
Collegiate Christian Union (OICCU) which opposed itself
to the "Marxist" Student Christian Movement. OICCs were

as fanatical as the Socialist Labour League Trotskyists, headed up locally by George Myers and Alan Clinton.

The year before I had arrived, Thornton-Duesbery had published a defence of Moral Re-Armament (MRA) against the criticisms of Tom Driberg, a Left Wing Labour MP, and this may be his Principal Publication. MRA had a dodgy history, like every American evangelical movement, and its founder Frank Buchman was perceived to have been soft in the 1930s on Fascism and Nazism. Now we begin to get to the point.

In the first place, as an unbeliever, I had had to identify myself as an outsider the moment I arrived at St Peter's. I could never be a "College Man" and I have only ever attended one College reunion - I tried hard but the weekend get-together incorporated no less than five periods of religious observance.

More importantly, the College statutes make no reference to "research" but rather to "education, religion and learning". Thornton-Duesbery was not an academic either in the sense it was then understood and even more so as it is understood now. He was a clergyman (one might say, a hereditary clergyman - his father, another Evangelical, was Bishop of Sodor and Man). And the fellows of St Peter's - the academic staff - included other men who were not obviously academics. There was a full time Chaplain, funded on the books, and there was Claude Wingfield Hope Sutton.

Claude Sutton interviewed me, rather sleepily, for my place at St Peter's. I remember he asked me a question about Nazism and Fascism. Only later did I discover that his interests in those subjects had been - as it were - practical rather than academic. In 1936 he had published *Farewell to Rousseau: a critique of liberal democracy.* It was rumoured that he had been interned in the War as a Nazi. I can find no Google evidence and I have since been told by a family member that he was questioned but not interned. He did publish articles in journals like *Philosophy* which are now academic but which in the 1940s and 1950s were more like journals of elevated opinion.

So one reason for St Peter's abysmal league table position was the fact that as a Private Hall up to 1961 it had pre-occupied itself with right-wing religion and politics and had a staff (now paid from public funds) which still partly reflected that fact. The 1961 move probably reflected financial distress rather than a desire to change its general character.

Jump forward nearly 50 years. St. Peter's has recently (2015) been named and shamed by the Government as one of the Oxford colleges with the worst records for admitting students from state school backgrounds. This surprised me. It was a College which had everything to gain from being more open than private clubs like Christ Church. But it is consistent with the claim, now regularly made, that the kind of social mobility which characterised the two or three decades after the Second World War, and from which I benefitted, has now come to an end.

The Poisoned Chalice

That social mobility did have characteristic disadvantages. You ceased to belong where you came from and you never quite belonged where you arrived. I was reminded of that again when British Prime Minister David Cameron was in trouble for things he is supposed to have done as a student at Oxford, allegedly sticking his cock in a dead pig's mouth - though only as part of an all-male Fraternity Club (that's American, I know) initiation ceremony. It reminded me of my only encounter with Frat Club ceremonies.

In the autumn of 1967, still an undergraduate at Oxford, I sat two examinations - traditional sit-downs with unseen papers and invigilators. But they weren't ordinary exams. You volunteered yourself for them (though you had to have a tutor's support) because they led to the award of University Prizes with prize money attached, £100 apiece. In one exam, you had three hours to answer just one question. I chose "Is Economic Growth a Good Thing?" which was a hot topic then and had been the subject of a recent (1966) book, *Is Economic Growth a Good Thing?* by E J Mishan. I had read it.

Anyway, I ended up the winner of the Junior George Webb Medley Prize in Economics and the Gibbs Prize in Politics. To win one Prize was regarded as a distinction. It was announced in The Times ("Henry" Anderson wrote me his congratulations) and it was recorded on your Degree certificate. Winning the two was almost unprecedented – I think I was the second person to do it. It was probably a tragic result for me, confirming me in an arrogant sense of my own abilities.

Shortly after winning I received an invitation to a Frat Club meeting. Not one devoted to sex, drugs and trashing restaurants (the sort you need to belong to if you want to become Prime Minister) but one devoted to elevated intellectual pursuits - a club where members met and listened to a paper and ate a meal. I guess it was Oxford's answer to the Cambridge Apostles. I can't remember the club's name.

The Club did meet in the same college as hosted some of

the more boisterous fraternities, Christ Church. I went along, recognised a few people but not many, listened to the paper. Then we ate. And then the Chalice was passed round. Everyone sipped from it and uttered the words "Church and Queen". The chalice arrived in my hands (nice bit of silverware) and I recall being watched closely. I passed the chalice to the person next to me. I didn't do Church and I didn't do Queen. I still don't. I never heard from the Frat Club again.

Time Mismanagement

W<small>E</small> all know what Time Management is. It's about making the best use of the finite amount of time available to us. It's not just about work time; it's about how we live our lives. When a book or a Time Management course – or just our own realisation – alerts us to the fact that it's possible to walk and chew gum at the same time, that's a liberating and empowering moment. It's the source of huge satisfaction to get a lot done in a day and, likewise, to complete a demanding work project without sacrificing the time we want to spend on other things. I don't need to elaborate. It's all familiar stuff. But our personal Time Management takes place in a social and political context. The trouble is this, that there are people and organisations out there determined to waste our time, big time. And I'm not just thinking about Passport Control. It's not just people and organisations, it's a background structure which we too easily take for granted.

Consider the almost universal institution of *Public Holidays*. These are days on which governments require or advise employers to lock out their workers. At a stroke, governments thereby deny many employees the possibility of time-managing a part of their (valuable) holiday time – often a significant part, since public holidays may constitute a quarter or more of an individual's annual holiday entitlement. The employees most affected are those in the public sector. Nor do different holidays affect different groups of workers: shops always stay open for locked-out public sector workers but there is never a day when supermarkets close and Town Halls stay open.

The most obvious fact about public holidays is that they lead to overloads on public transport systems. Instead of enjoying their time off work, people end up in queues of one kind or another. And though the committed Time Manager will find something else to do when in a queue, even if only chewing gum, this is going to be a second-best use of valuable time. There are other frustrations. Here in the UK, Public Holidays have never really responded to any popular sense that "This is when we would all like a day off together". Instead, to take the worst example, Easter is dumped on us and, however much it is moved about by the astrologers, it always seems to coincide with bad weather. Google "Bank Holiday Washout" and you get a downpour of results.

So however good our personal Time Management may be, Public Holidays are pretty much a kick in the teeth. It's worse in countries where they are compulsory; in the UK, they are merely advisory – the Department of Business publishes the annual List of Days. The Prime Minister is entitled to interfere with the List, like some school Speech Day grandee, adding Days Off to make us stay at home and watch Royal Weddings. But he never adds days for football matches or Valentine's Day or Bonfire Night.

The two public holidays which are actually popular in the UK do not need official protection. Charles Dickens' *A Christmas Carol* protects Christmas Day from Scrooge, and even the Scrooges of this world do not want their workers turning up hung over on 1st January so they will shut up shop of their own accord. What is ridiculous in the United Kingdom, and not copied anywhere else in Europe, is the convention (insisted upon by Public Sector Trade Unions) that if New Year's Day falls on a Saturday or Sunday, then the following Monday should be a Public Holiday. That's the kind of thing which makes public holidays frustrating for many workers, who end up locked out when they would be happy to work and made to work when they would prefer to take a holiday.

The economic benefits from abolishing public holidays would be enormous – occasional attempts have been made to quantify it - and would certainly justify increasing the minimum holiday entitlement for a full time worker on a standard five day week. Even if that minimum was set as low as 30 days, that allows for two breaks of a week each and one long break of four. But there would be workers who would prefer to take off 30 Fridays or Mondays and thus give themselves 30 three day Short Break weekends. In these things, there is no need for one size to fit all.

Public Holidays are the paradigm case of organisational mismanagement of other people's time. Holidays are things which people have a good claim to manage for themselves, agreeing their time off with employers. It would only be a challenge for those government offices which have never heard of the word *Rota* and those Unions which specialise in creating nudge-and-a-wink double-time and treble-time working for favoured members who come in on the Saturday to do the work missed on the Monday and who think that such crooked schemes are preferable to higher pay rates all round.

*

Other examples of time mismanagement are more complicated and vary between countries.

In the UK, the very long-term and utterly abysmal failure of governments to have recognisable housing policies or transport policies has condemned workers, especially in the London hub, to longer *Home to Work Commuting Times* than are found in other advanced economies.

Now for sure there are those who will insist that they would resist any reduction in their commuting time below the number of minutes needed to finish the crossword. But in truth, for most workers commuting time is better shorter. You can try to multi-task on the daily commute and many succeed, but it's always a bit forced. As a result, sixty minutes commuting bad; twenty minutes good. It would be highly desirable for governments to have as a general policy the aim of cutting average Home to Work commuting times. That would really improve quality of life for millions of people, because it would free up time for more productive and enjoyable activity.

Of course, to a reader in southern England, the idea of working towards a Commuting Time target will sound Utopian. It is clearly beyond the wit of the kind of governments the UK is blessed with that housing policies and transport policies should be co-ordinated to get people closer to their place of work (or vice versa). Some people would say that it is beyond the capacity of any government. Policy would require endless tuning and re-tuning and though that's possible for interest rates, infrastructure can't be continuously re- configured. But if, for example, London had a regional government rather than a glorified Town Council it might be possible to get the idea on the agenda. That isn't going to happen because central government needs London tax revenues to prop up the loss-making subsidiaries of Northern Ireland, Northern England and Wales. A London regional government would almost certainly try to thwart those central government purposes. As Mayor of London, Boris Johnson did indeed cause trouble by suggesting that Stamp Duty on London house sales should go to his own council.

London's relation to the UK government is itself something worth thinking about. Central government in the UK is an organisation which camps in London but has no feel for it. That's why when Parliament opens each year, governments think nothing of closing off London streets for the State Opening of Parliament. So what if people, on an ordinary working day, are inconvenienced by yet more pointless, ostentatious pomp?

*

Public Holidays, Commuting Time. These are key areas where public policy or the lack of it wastes private time. As a third example, consider *The Clocks*. It falls to government to synchronise our watches, to set the time. It is government which solves this co-ordination problem. Unfortunately, the UK government chooses a solution which suits the Highlands of Scotland and nowhere else in Britain, setting the clocks one hour behind those of our near neighbours in continental Europe. There are compelling reasons for thinking that south of the Scottish border the clocks should be aligned with those of Europe (one hour ahead of their current setting). All the evidence is that road accidents would be reduced if Autumn and Winter afternoon darkness was not thrust upon us an hour earlier than necessary. More daylight at the end of the working day would save lives. In addition, more daylight after work and school increases the range of things which people (including children) can do with their time. More light enables people to get more satisfaction from their time. Governments have no enthusiasm for that.

*

As a final very complicated example consider *Weekends*. These are deeply embedded in European cultures. Whatever their origins, they now function in a remarkably discriminatory way, rather like Public Holidays. There are workers who always get a break from Friday afternoon to Monday morning and workers who never do because they are employed in sectors which serve those on their weekend break. The dysfunctionality of the system manifests itself in many ways – weekend traffic jams (originally satirised in Jean-Luc Godard's 1967 film *Weekend*) and the fact that if you are admitted to hospital at the weekend you are more likely to die because senior medical staff have cleared off for the regular break to which their social status entitles them.

Just as we could live better without public holidays it may well be that we could live better without weekends, making even more extensive use of rota systems which ensured that everyone could benefit from regular two or three day work breaks if they wanted. It would require some imaginative re-thinking (aided by a very powerful computer) of how we manage our lives and would come up against obvious problems: what would happen to Saturday football matches? How are families to get together if they don't have their time off at the same time? What about schools? But those are already significant problems for very many workers in sectors like retail and catering who at present are treated as too low in the social hierarchy for their experience to count in the formulation of public policy.

My overall sense is that we could do so much better than we do at the moment in managing Public Time, if only governments felt obliged to spare some time to re-organising it. First, though, step forward a policy think tank to produce a stirring Report.

Universal Suffrage

THE campaign slogan was never "One Person One Vote" or even "One Adult One Vote" but always "One Man One Vote". Most people think that their countries had a functioning democracy even before the vote was extended to women - everyone knows that in Europe Switzerland got there last (in 1971). Of those who fought and died in the trenches of the First World War, few believed in votes for women and fewer that women should be there in the trenches beside them.

There were other, lesser anomalies than the exclusion of women: in the United Kingdom, the Property Owner's Vote and the Universities Vote gave some people two votes. If you graduated from the universities of Cambridge or Oxford, you got an extra vote to use in electing an MP for your old University. That inequality was only abolished in 1948. Some adults don't get the vote - in the UK, prisoners, and in other times and places, lunatics and bankrupts. No one in politics suggests that children should have the vote, though in my life time the voting age has been reduced from 21 to 18 and for the Scottish independence referendum it was reduced to 16 to try to weight things in favour of those who might think more about the future than the past. But for the BREXIT referendum in 2016, younger voters were very deliberately excluded.

So Universal Suffrage is a bit variable as is the Majoritarian principle: in both the USA and the UK, you can win an election outright with fewer votes than a single opponent. George W Bush did it first time around in 2000 (repeating a scenario from 1824, 1827 and 1888) and the Conservatives did it in 1951 Britain: in the latter (undisputed) case, Churchill's Conservatives polled 13 717 850 votes and won 321 seats; Clement Attlee's Labour 13 948 385 for 295 seats; the Liberals on six seats did not hold a balance of power nor did anyone else. Those are not insignificant anomalies in systems where Winner Takes All, but so weak is the public's commitment to Majoritarianism that no one rioted against a *coup d'état*. Other systems are less perverse, Germany's notably - that country up to 2016 has been run for an extended period on a fairly steady course steered by a Grand Coalition (the Germans call it a *GroKo*) of parties.

It's relevant that, in most cases, major things we associate with democracy like a free press and freedom from arbitrary arrest were in place before the arrival of universal suffrage. Think only of the Swiss case. In ex-colonial and other liberated countries where universal suffrage has been introduced first, a free press and so on do not always follow: universal suffrage on its own does not make a democracy.

All the history of the fight for the Vote took place against a very particular demographic background, a world of young people and working people. Life expectancies in the major democracies meant that the elderly - the retired, pensioners, the elderly frail - were a small part of the population. The significance of this fact has generally been overlooked. It gave a forward-looking bias to democratic politics, sometimes disastrous for democracy itself (Fascism, Nazism).

Now the situation has changed and the increasingly elderly demographic of the advanced democracies, and even more so of active voters, gives a backward-looking bias to their politics. British political parties lack a vision for the future because they are not responding to voters who are seeking such a vision. They are responding to voters who want the past and whose time horizon is at best the next few years. They look backwards, not forwards, and in terms of narrowly selfish preoccupations, they win hands down. They want to know what's in it for them and that's about it - apart from some xenophobia. They dominate elections so totally now that younger people don't bother to vote and people who don't own their own homes don't bother to vote either. Those two self-excluding categories heavily overlap. They know that the political parties aren't interested in them. It's a bad situation to be in. We should be much more wary of the electoral gerontocracy. There is no obvious reason why this situation should be accepted. Some means of curbing the destructive power of elderly voters is needed.

We treat it as natural that children should not have the vote - we don't think of them as disenfranchised. However, occasionally it has been proposed that parents should get extra votes for dependent children, in order to increase the importance of long-term planning as an election issue. The idea was put forward by the UK think tank Demos in 2003, by the Dutch economist Lans Bovenberg in 2007 and it is an official policy of the Christian Party of Austria. In addition or as an alternative, we should think about whether elderly people should have the vote or the full vote. Maybe the vote is something you should get at 18 and keep until you are 68 or, subject to fitness, 78 or 88. A bit like a driving licence. Maybe it is something which should reduce in value as the decades pass, so that a full vote at 18 becomes a half vote at 68 and so on down.

At a stroke, this would change the whole electoral situation and would force the sclerotic political parties to confront a whole range of issues they would prefer to duck. Housing would be the obvious one, where at the moment the main voter priority is to keep house prices rising, but others would include drugs policy, jobs, energy supply, transport infrastructure and climate change. That's just for starters. They might even have to think about their cosy little assumption that next comes King Charles III. Oh I know these are outrageous ideas. But think about it. Do you really want to be ruled by the dead souls of *The Daily Express*?

Vices & Virtues

THE Seven Deadly Sins were never listed on any tablet of stone but evolved along with the history of organised Christianity and eventually settled down to Envy, Gluttony, Greed, Lust, Pride, Sloth and Wrath. I imagine ill-tempered committees of the not-so-great-and-good venting their spleen over the centuries:

We need to clamp down on these peasants. Forgetting their place nowadays! Full of sloth! Put that on the list!

And another thing, they're at it all the time. No decency, no self-control, lusting after each other and laughing at us! Put that on the list!

I ask myself, What do I think of as Deadly Sins, sins which pitch people down the slippery slope towards perdition?

First, there are *Sins against the Self*. I recoil from *Self-Pity* and *Self-Neglect* which show lack of *Self-Respect* or - in other words – lack of *Pride* (one of the Deadlies). The slings and arrows of outrageous fortune will always wound us, but with self-respect, not so deeply. Lose your Pride, and you have stopped saying Yes to life and its possibilities, including the possibility of doing good in this world. So

Pride protects us from the sins of self-pity and self-neglect. It gives us dignity. It's roughly what Rousseau called *amour de soi,* love of oneself, which he distinguishes from *amour propre* which is vanity.

Then there are *Sins against Others.* The Church proposes Temperance and Chastity as the Virtues which protect us from the sins of Gluttony and Lust. But Christian temperance does not always take the benign form of eating your Five a Day. It turns into Meanness, which is a lack of generosity towards the world. And Chastity as well as having no obvious moral merit often turns into Prudery, which is the vice of disapproving of one's fellow human beings – something of which you can make a full-time job. *Meanness* and *Prudery* are Sins from which *Gluttony* and *Lust* afford some protection.

In a wonderful film *Babette's Feast* (Gabriel Axel, 1987), it is the experience of Gluttony which humanises the Biblical sectarians. The refugee cook who they have employed out of Christian Charity (topped off with self-interest) receives news that she has won the Lottery back in the repressive France from which she has fled. When the money arrives, she blows the lot on a single feast offered to her employers and their fellow church members. They are seduced by *haute cuisine* into the experience of enjoyment and they are morally improved by that experience: their pleasure allows them to connect with the virtues of benevolence, forgiveness and generosity. It's not just a good story for a film either: empirical studies show that judges hand down more lenient sentences after they have had lunch.

In the life of Oskar Schindler, it is his Lust which ensures that his heart is not locked against his fellow human beings.

This is something which the 2004 biography *Oskar Schindler* by David M Crowe doesn't comprehend. The biographer simply can't handle Schindler and ends up in the odd position of trying to ignore what he was. (Steven Spielberg's 1993 film *Schindler's List* is better in this respect). The thing about Schindler is this, that you can throw at his character a dozen negative epithets and they help explain the facts that he had a huge life-affirming capacity for bravery and humanity and that, when the chips were down, he accepted the unsought challenge his situation presented to him. It wasn't even his duty: he displayed what the specialists in these things used to call superogatory virtue. Voluntarily, he did more good work than the minimum required by whatever Rules of Right Conduct applied to his situation.

It is often remarked that the Seven Deadlies do not include *Cruelty* (*Wrath* certainly does not encompass it). But *Cruelty* is the sin which most brutally disfigures human relationships. It is an exercise of power: of parents against their children; of the Church against heretics; of despots against their "people" - and it gets passed down the line and from generation to generation. In Ireland and Italy, the cruelty of the Church disfigured whole societies - and, oh, in what whining Self-Pity that Church now indulges when anyone tries to hold it to account. The virtues which oppose themselves to Cruelty are Kindness or Benevolence or, simply, Love. The Church got one thing right.

It is also remarked that *Dishonesty* is not among the Seven Deadlies. Maybe the Committee responsible for the final cut of the List had their hands in the collection plate. But I also hesitate to include dishonesty on my own List. It's sometimes cruel (so it can be dealt with under that head) but more often it's merely tiresome. I don't want to go to the wall on it, but I am inclined to think *Hypocrisy* a greater Sin than dishonesty because it is what so often cements societies around things which, actually, no one believes in.

"Faith Schools" (an expression you will understand better if you think of its twin, "Respectable Brothels") can *only* exist in my country because most teachers are willing to keep their mouths shut about what they believe (or more often, don't believe). The core *ethos* of a modern Faith School is one where the Governors know that most of their teachers do not share the Faith but appoint them because there is *literally no one else* and the wrong-faith or faithless teachers know that they are expected to keep quiet about this situation (and, to their shame, often do so). And the pupils, of course, always know what's going on: it is their traditional role to spot the Emperor's Clothes. The virtue which protects us from hypocrisy in ourselves is Pride and from hypocrisy in others, Wrath. Oh, how those *teachers* deserve a tongue lashing for what they go along with!

Greed and *Envy* complete the traditional list of the Seven Deadlies, a double whammy aimed at the poor who might otherwise get it into their heads to take a share of the landlord's or the bishop's wealth, forgetting that the world is only rightly ordered when the rich man is in his castle and the poor man at his gate ("God made them high and lowly and ordered their estate" – words from the all-time chart-topping Church of England hymn for little children, *All Things Bright and Beautiful*, got up by Mrs Cecil Alexander in 1848).

I don't like Envy. I think it's an unpleasant personality trait and I don't blame defenders of the rich when they play the Envy card: I would, since it's a strong card to play. The irrationality of envy is shown by the fact that it is something which never yields to bribery – give the envious person something and they just move on to the next thing to be envious about. Greed is less insidious. In the specific form of Gluttony I find it charming. It's so childlike, so innocent. Ask me for Relationship advice, and one of my tips would be to avoid anyone who is picky about their food. Go for a glutton! They are less likely to chastise you for your shortcomings. Other forms of Greed don't greatly trouble me emotionally and sometimes they are simply comic. Imelda Marcos will be remembered forever as the woman with a wardrobe of shoes. It's not really the way you want to be remembered, is it?

But I am clear in my mind that Greed, though in appearance innocuous, has to be legislated against. I believe in the Minimum Wage but also in the Maximum Wage and I would legislate for both. I am happy to take my cue from the economist Thomas Piketty (in a 2015 conversation with a *Financial Times* journalist) and propose that the Maximum should be set at 20 times the Median salary. So if the median is £25 000 then the Maximum is £500 000. I think I am taking my cue from anti-poverty campaigners if I set the Minimum at 60% of the Median, so £15 000. There is plenty of room in that spread for some people to have aspirations and some to have lots of shoes. To keep things egalitarian, you also need inheritance taxes which constantly level the playing field between generations. But philanthropy can do some of the work too: there are lots of rich people who like to give away money and more will enjoy giving away if they know that otherwise it will be taken away.

All the evidence - start with the fine 2009 book, *The Spirit Level* by Richard Wilkinson and Kate Pickett, the best of the bunch when it comes to books on equality and inequality - adds up to the general conclusion that more equal societies have less crime, less violence, have happier and healthier citizens, don't have to waste money on gating communities, and such like. They are economically successful too. In general, they are societies where governments take more of national product in taxes – the Scandinavian countries notably – but in one important case (Japan) they don't. If you legislate for Minimum and Maximum Wages, adopting a policy of what is called *pre-distribution* then you don't need the big government bureaucracies which *re-distribute* money from rich to poor and you will avoid the social evil of benefit dependency. It's not obligatory to take this line, and it may be that maximum wages are most easily enforced through high marginal tax rates like those the USA and UK had under Republican and Conservative governments in the 1950s and 1960s, but in principle you can – like me - be both an egalitarian and at the same time believe in a small(er) state.

War & Terror

EVERYONE knows that in the First World War, the imperial governments of Europe – the dual monarchy of Austria and Hungary, Britain, France, Germany, Russia, Turkey - sent millions of conscripted young men into the horrific slaughter of trench warfare. In the aftermath, their successors knew that they simply did not have the manpower left to do it again and so looked to aerial warfare as an alternative. They were also conscious that they might be strung up from the lamp posts if they tried for another trench war. Britain and France could point to the territory they had gained from the slaughter – virtually the whole of the Middle East, parts of Africa – but only ardent imperialists, the people in Westminster and the Elysée, thought that this justified the price paid. Even before the great powers had the bombers, they thought that the next war ought to be about strategic bombing from the air. Only the Soviet Union thought that air power should be used, almost exclusively, to give tactical support to ground forces. Over the next eighty years, the UK and then the US perfected the technology and techniques of attacking civilians from a great height over Germany, then Japan, Korea, Vietnam, Laos, Cambodia and most recently Iraq, Afghanistan and Syria.

At the end of his 800 plus page but very readable 2013 book *The Bombing War: Europe 1939 - 1945*, Richard

Overy - drawing on a mountain of statistical information and military analysis - concludes that in the Second World War governments condemned half a million European civilians to mostly pointless slaughter as bombs fell on them.

The pointlessness had two main aspects. First - and this is true for American bombing - the bombers could not hit their intended targets. Time after time – because of technological limitations, the weather, human error - they missed. Instead of hitting factories or transport links, they hit residential quarters. At times, pilots under pressure to off-load simply gave up even trying to bomb on target. Reading Overy, I was repeatedly surprised at the very low percentages achieved for "on target" bombs. Aircraft loss percentages were sometimes higher than percentages for on-target bombs.

Second - and this is true for British bombing - when bombers were sent to carpet bomb cities, they either failed to do it (came home, got shot down, bombed rural fields) or else, where they were successful, as at Hamburg and Dresden, did not achieve their aim of breaking enemy civilian morale or crippling industry through killing workers in their beds. At the time, assessment of success in fulfilling the strategic task assigned to Britain's Bomber Command was confused by the bluster of its Commander in Chief, Sir Arthur Harris. The bombs available to the man happy with his nickname, Bomber Harris, were just not capable of doing the job which the bombs available in 1945 did to Nagasaki and Hiroshima. On the other side, neither the Germans and still less the Italians who were supposed to do the job, found a way of bombing the small island of Malta - hardly missable as a target in the open Mediterranean - into submission.

In other words, strategic bombing did not bring victory or end the war faster, with just one qualification: in all the belligerent countries, exposure to bombing tied up large numbers of personnel and a great deal of materiel in air raid defences. But that concession is not such a big one: all the belligerents had this hand tied behind their backs so none of them gained an advantage over the other.

In passing, Richard Overy mentions a 1931 book by H G Wells, *The Shape of Things to Come* which "ends optimistically with a benign world 'Air Dictatorship' based implausibly in the Iraqi city of Basra" (page 31). Perhaps not so implausibly.

*

In 1918, Britain took Iraq from the collapsed Ottoman Empire in a deal with the French which gave them Syria and Lebanon. Britain also took Palestine. These new colonies were held under a fig-leaf League of Nations "Mandate" which looked to the hand-over of these territories to local control when the Natives were ready for self-government. There is a very good account of the deal, the so-called Sykes-Picot agreement of 1917 and its consequences over the following decades, in James Barr's 2012 book, *A Line in the Sand*.

It was in Iraq in the 1920s that Arthur Harris, of the occupying British forces, experimented with the technique of bombing civilians from the air to terrorise and break them. What he did there was controversial within the RAF itself and attracted adverse publicity which Wells may have been familiar with. There is an account of what Harris did in Iraq in the 2010 collection *Bombing Civilians* edited by

Yuki Tanaka and Marilyn Young. Here, for example, is an extract from a 1924 report by Harris which appears at page 21 of that book:

> *They [the Arabs and Kurds] now know what real bombing means, in casualties and damage: they now know that within 45 minutes a full sized village, vide attached photos of Kushan-Al-Ajaza, can be practically wiped out and a third of its inhabitants killed or injured by four or five machines which offer them no real target, no opportunity for glory as warriors, no effective means of escape, and little chance of retaliation or loot such as an infantry column would afford them in producing a similar result*

These enthusiastic views were not immediately endorsed either by all politicians or all members of the RAF. Air Commodore Lionel Charlton, chief air staff officer in Baghdad, voiced disquiet. He drew attention to the inaccuracy of the bombs being used, the faulty intelligence that led to them being dropped in the wrong places, and the horrific injuries to civilians which resulted (he visited hospitals). Charlton resigned his Iraq post and subsequently in 1928 was forced out or took early retirement from the RAF (Tanaka and Young pp 23 – 24; the accounts of Charlton's fate differ between sources).

But most politicians and certainly those in power saw aerial bombing, openly described as a terror technique, as a way to reduce their own military casualties almost to zero. Dropping bombs on uncivilised tribespeople played better with electorates than putting troops in the line of fire. It still does. The technology still regularly blasts to bits patients in hospitals and children in schools. When in 2015 the Russians joined in on the bombing of Syria they immediately proved to be very good at firing their missiles inaccurately. Nothing seems to change. And with the exception of Japan in 1945, none of it can claim to have worked. Even the horrific American carpet bombing and napalming of Indo-China failed: today a unified and modestly prosperous Vietnam has as its capital Ho Chi Minh City. Cambodia and Laos are still there.

Here in Europe and the USA, people watching the News or reading the newspapers do not any longer have to think of what their governments do as terrorism; we have been cleansed of the candour of Arthur "Bomber" Harris. To us, terrorism is the preserve of people who don't have our kind of bombs and missiles but who rather terrifyingly kill themselves at the same time as they kill a few of us. But when it comes to the kill count, we are way out in front, so much so that we do not even bother to do the counting. A toll that takes terrorists a year to achieve, we can pile up in an hour. And gathering up the body parts and burying them is simply someone else's problem.

X & the Alphabet

AT first, I thought I would have to 'fess up that I don't have anything to say about xeroxes or xylophones or even xenophobia, nor about X-Rays, X-Films or X-Factors. Then I thought I had a way in through the fine 2007 Argentinian film *XXY* which is about the difficult experience of hermpahroditism – intersex nowadays – and about which I thought I had something to say. But my editor simply wrote at the end of my effort "I'm not sure this earns its place in the book". That's what editors are for, unfortunately. So it was back to the writing board. And then I realised that the problem is with the letter X and that you could write an interesting book about how and why it's a problem and to prove that, well, all I have to do is write the preliminary outline of that book here.

It goes like this. The letter X does not pull its weight in the alphabet. There are only 26 letters in the English alphabet and they have their work cut out to represent a million words. How come X is still in a job when it manages to start off only one hundred or so words, most of which we don't know anyway? And those hundred or so words could all be started off with a Z quite satisfactorily (*zeroxes, zylophones, zenophobia*). It's as if the team is a player short.

Well, in its defence, you could say that it has found a second job working as an adjective rather than a letter, fronting up hyphenated words like X-ray and what would normally be hyphenated words like xbox. This is true but not exclusive to X: we have B-movies and G-forces. As a second line of defence, you could point out that at the end of words X does another grammatical job indicating that a word is singular rather than plural:

box, cox, fox, pox … are all singular, though they would sound the same if spelt *bocks, cocks, focks, pocks,* and those are at the same time versions which can cope with a plural, so *fockses* instead of *foxes* is at least as transparent.

cocks, docks, locks, socks …. under the present regime, words ending in *cks* are always plurals. The proof of this is demonstrated by the fact that we know that *sox* as an alternative plural of *sock* (as in *Bobby sox*) is just a gimmick.

But this idea that X is doing work for grammar is dubious; it makes it sound like X is moonlighting twice over, just because it has only a part-time job as a letter of the alphabet.

You may be inclined to persist in defence of X and I think that might be because somehow you just feel that a letter of the alphabet surely must be *fit for purpose*. If it wasn't, it would have been eliminated long ago. Well, that's a popular neo-Darwinian way of thinking which used to be summarised in the expression (or eckspression) *The Survival of the Fittest*. In turn, that doctrine connects to a smiley-faced version of the same idea, *All is for the Best in the Best of All Possible Worlds* – interfere at your peril.

The *All Is for the Best* doctrine is clearly ludicrous and the idea that everything in the world is fully fitted to purpose and can't be improved on – the fancy name for this idea is *eufunctionalism* – is falsified by such simple observations as this: the fact that all the cars on the road today are being driven around does not prove that they are all in equally good running order. Likewise, just because the letter X is there in the alphabet being taught every day in school does not mean that it is in as good shape as A or B. Frankly, it's struggling.

At this point the story ought to shift to the task of explaining what you might call the *Persistence of X.* Let's start with a story. If you build a house in brick on clay soil then spontaneous movements in the terrain you have chosen can be greater than your house can tolerate so that the walls crack – maybe only a little – and the house subsides – maybe only a little. You have put a lot of money into the house and so you put up with the problems unless they become so big that the rain starts coming in or the walls actually start falling down. It's not what you desire, it's not your preferred state to be living in this house with cracks in the walls. You know it's less than the best of all possible worlds. It's sub-optimal and in time it may really become not fit for purpose. But you may still be living in it. And there may be no easy way out. Lots of people actually experience such situations.

Now switch from the story to a metaphor. Written languages and the alphabets that enable them are not built on clay but are surrounded by an ocean of spoken language, constantly moving and shifting. Spoken language is liable to unending and sometimes quite rapid changes, some of them very difficult to describe and explain. You can't turn them away, any more than you can turn back the waves. Written languages and alphabets float on this ocean. They would not exist without it but their relation to it is changing, uncertain and sometimes disastrous. Spellings change a bit to reflect, after the event, what has happened to intonation or pronunciation - in English in the recent past *Rumania* and *Roumania* have given way to *Romania* . But alphabets barely change at all and then only over extended periods of time. Alphabets may end up having nothing to do with spoken language and, for some languages, that is quite true or partly true. The alphabet we know connects better to spoken Italian than it does to spoken English, for instance, which may have something to do with the fact that it's a Latin (Roman) alphabet and Italian is even now a Latin (Romance) language. English isn't. It just happens to be represented through the alphabet of Britain's former colonial masters.

Certainly, alphabets – like QWERTY keyboards - are structurally rigid in the sense that it is hard to interfere with one element without disrupting the whole. In addition, alphabets solve a co-ordination problem, ensuring we all behave the same way when there is no obvious right way. So it becomes one of those cases where we really need a government to order a change and ensure that we all follow its lead and, ideally, at the same time. That is, for example, usually the only way you can change from driving on the left to driving on the right. Sweden made the change as late as 1967 and it's an interesting story. Another story is a bit different. Czechoslovakia's government had already committed to switching from driving on the left to driving on the right when the country was occupied by Germany in 1939. As a result, the planned transition was accelerated by the simple fact that German military traffic entered the country on the right hand side of the road and stayed there. In some places every driver had switched within 24 hours and, in the country as a whole, the changeover triggered by *force majeure* was completed within a fortnight and with one fatality.

As another example of changing a co-ordination arrange-ment, it took the Russian Revolution to impose a more accurate calendar – in Bolshevik Russia, the changeover took place in 1918 with 31 January followed by 14 February. I have a card from a Danish traveller in Omsk writing home on the 14th February and noting that it's for the first time the same date in both Russia and Denmark. In the early revolutionary period the Soviets also edited the Russian alphabet and spelling, sending in the military to confiscate from printers the type used to set the abolished hard sign. In both cases, change was seen both as a pre-requisite for entering the modern era and as the enforcement of rationality.

We stick with the creaking cultural technology of our old alphabet as with so much else. True, it's preferable to blood-shed. And, true, that with the arrival of the Internet it would probably now take a world government to change it. But it takes its toll. In British primary schools, there is this thing called Phonics, the product of our best brains and industry, which launches all right on A and B but promptly gets sea-sick on curly C and kicking K (I think that's called re-arranging the deckchairs) before drowning in X. For school children, it's a voyage on the *Titanic*. The survivors are those who manage – probably with parental help - to climb overboard in time. (If you are a parent and want to explore how Phonics is working for your child, here's a suggestion: When their next birthday comes round, ask them to write down for you the names of the friends they want to invite. Maybe you will have to help and sound out for them, but this time no cheating to turn *a – n* into *Anna* and so on down the list and fingers crossed that there is no one in class called Xavier).

As I promised, there's a book here and an Internet very willing to help you write it.

Young Girl with a Fan?

THE spirit of political correctness is the desire for societies less discriminatory, less prejudiced, more just and fairer. The letter of political correctness has often enough cramped that into bureaucratic procedures or rules. The letter of the law is almost always a poor guide. All purely bureaucratic procedures, however well-motivated, can and do fail to give justice to the individual case and even, at worst, repeat an injustice they were supposed to remedy. That is the argument I want to illustrate in this little study.

*

In January 1921, an Amsterdam diamond dealer Andries van Wezel, died on board the *S.S. Rotterdam* en route from New York to the Netherlands. He was wealthy, a prominent Dutch Jew, a philanthropist and an art collector. He bequeathed his large collection of around 140 paintings and drawings to Amsterdam's Rijksmuseum. In among many more valuable or important works was a small (41 x 29 cm portrait format) oil on canvas painting signed by and attributed to a contemporary Dutch painter and art dealer, Simon Maris (1873 – 1935), the son of a landscape painter, Willem Maris. The painting is reproduced on the inside back cover of this book.

In 1922, the Rijksmuseum staff - working their way through the bequest - inventoried and catalogued this painting under a title which they provided themselves, *Negerinnetje*, which is sometimes translated to English as "Little Negress" and sometimes as "Young Negro Girl". The former translation is an older one, since the recent history of both American and British English has led to the progressive disappearance of the " – ess" forms to indicate a female: so "actress" has given way to "actor", "authoress" [which never had much currency] to "author" and so on. Likewise, "Negress" has no currency now.

The form "Young ... girl" (and its twin, "Young ... boy") is a bit odd in English since it is unclear what "young" changes in "girl" or "boy". Perhaps it indicates to the listener to think "pre-puberty" or something like that, but I am not sure – it isn't clearly wrong in many contexts to call a fifteen year old a "young girl" or "young boy". It is quite important to note that Dutch "Neger" and "Negerin" do not translate to American "Nigger"; they translate to American and British "Negro". The diminutive " – etje" ending does the job done in English by "Little" and "Young".

One hundred years later, Google the word which some museum curator picked for the title of the Maris painting and, well, you get an awful lot of Dutch porn sites (there is a negerinnetjes.tube.nl) but you also get some Facebook-type family images of children(female, black) under the age of about 10. This surprised me because I had expected that, as in American and English, "black" would have completely won out over "Negro" as a clearly non-offensive term of choice. "Black" does exist in Dutch, with a phrase like "Jonge zwarte vrouw" available as a neutral description. However - and this is relevant for what follows - "Jonge zwarte vrouw" can translate as both "young black woman" and "young black girl" even though Dutch does have a separate word for girl ("meisje" – the etymology would link it to German "Mädchen" and English "maiden")

*

At the end of 2015, Amsterdam's Rijksmuseum announced that it was in the process of re-titling hundreds of works in its (vast) collection which had racist or, more generally, offensive or Eurocentric titles. One curator, Eveline Sint Nicolaas, was interviewed by Patrick Meeershoek for *Het Parool* which published the story on 9 December; the head of the history department, Martine Gosselink, spoke to Nina Siegal of the *New York Times* which published on 10 December. The latter interview is illustrated with the Simon Maris painting. Since then, the story has been carried in news media in many countries. After all, most countries have art museums and the Rijksmuseum project is probably relevant to all of them. As of early February 2016, the story had been carried by national newspapers and online media in Argentina, Brazil, Ecuador, France, Hungary, Indonesia, Italy, Poland, Romania, Spain, Switzerland, United Kingdom and USA. Most of them picked up on the *New York Times* version.

Martine Gosselink did refer to the difference between titles given by painters and titles given by galleries, but this does not come through clearly in the *New York Times* interview. Many if not most titles used to label works in galleries and museums have not been provided by the painter or sculptor. They are due entirely either to custom or, more likely, the curator who inventoried the work at the time of its acquisition. That is an important difference. If a painter gives a title to a work, it often has little or no more significance than an inventory title. Not all painters want to provide a verbal guide to their work. But sometimes they do and that is then an important fact. It tells you how the *painter* wants / wanted you to look at the work. So if the painter assigns an indicative title, *The Very Fat Man*, then the painter is saying to us (as it were): Look, start from the fact that he's very fat. Not from the fact that he's bald or black. Look at how I have tried to represent his fatness or – more subtly – how this fat man relates to his own fatness. In these circumstances, it would be a foolish curator who interposed and decided, No, we are not going to use that title (any more). We are going to re-title this painting *The Bald Headed Man* or *Man Sitting in an Armchair*. The first of these would privilege the curator's interpretation of the picture over the painter's. The second is, effectively, banal and simply removes the guidance provided by the original title. Or if it is not just banal, it is misleading if it leads us to ask questions like, *How does the man manage his relationship to the chair?* instead of the previous (possible) question, *How does the man manage his relation to his fatness?*

There will be occasions – perhaps numerous – where we conclude that even the painter's indications are uninteresting or unhelpful or simply express prejudices which the painting may not even confirm. There almost certainly exists a painting where the painter says *A Shifty-Eyed Thief* but where the spectator promptly dissents and thinks *A Thief pretending to be shifty-eyed to conform to your stereotypes...*

In other words, though an artist's title may in some sense

be intended to close down interpretation, it may not in fact do so. Painters do not have a monopoly of wisdom, even about their own work. Spectators may see more than the painter ever saw. But nonetheless, they probably want to start from where the painter started (why else look at paintings?) and if you remove *the painter's title*, then spectators are – with some justification - going to cry "Foul!" and "Anachronism!" and "Political Correctness Gone Mad!". And indeed they did in response to what they thought the Rijksmuseum was doing, even though in the initial phase of re-titling it has concentrated on gallery-given titles.

*

The accounts of the Rijksmuseum's project are almost identical across all the media coverage I noted above. (At first, I thought there was a single Press Release but there wasn't). And the painting which appears in nearly all the accounts is the image of Simon Maris's painting once given the title by a curator, *Negerinnetje*, and which now – thanks to this museum project entitled "Adjustment of Colonial Terminology" - had a shiny new curator title, *Jonge vrouw met waaier* which you can translate as either *Young Woman with a Fan* or *Young Girl with a Fan*. In context, "Young Girl" is more accurate as a translation since the Rijksmuseum on its website also grouped the painting under Children's Portraits (*Kinderportret*) and, in fact, the new English title chosen for the painting was "Young Girl with a Fan".

Since this is just the replacement of one curator title by another, one can ask quite simple questions about it. Does it help us see the painting for what it is (for what is intended)? Does it do better than the old title? I think the answer here is clearly, No. The world's art galleries are full of young girls with fans – you might say it is a trope of gallery rhetoric - and the new title is as banal as *Man Sitting in an Armchair*. If you start looking at this painting by looking at the fan, how the girl holds the fan, and so on – well, you are wasting your time. Galleries are not entirely to blame for this: so called "genre paintings" are, by their nature, difficult to title since they show – well – generic things like *Still Life with Apples*.

The new gallery labelling expanded on the title and added that this painting is dated as having been painted between 1895 and 1922 (the latter the date at which it arrived in the Rijksmuseum) and attributes it to the white Dutch painter and art dealer, Simon Maris, active between those dates. If that is correct, then just the smallest bit of historical knowledge will suggest to a spectator that more interesting than the fan is the fact that the sitter is black. Not only is she black, she is rather finely dressed and she is sitting rather confidently in her chair to be painted by a leading Dutch portrait painter of the time. You might at least expect a bit of curiosity about those facts. Not many black girls got to do those things then. The Rijksmuseum did acknowledge her blackness in a new longer description of the work, which I took from the Museum website shortly after the December 2105 adjusted title was published:

> *Een zittende jonge zwarte vrouw, met een kanten hoed op het hoofd en een waaier in de rechterhand*

which I translate as:

*A young black girl sitting, with a lace bonnet on her
head and a fan in her right hand*

Is that longer description good enough to get started on
looking at this painting? I think not.

*

I suggest that you will get more initial insight if you try
looking at her *left* hand which - as far as I can discover - no
one has previously proposed.

The sitter has been posed by the painter with her left hand
splayed so that it is easy to see that on the third finger of
her left hand she is wearing a ring. In European cultures,
the third finger of the left hand is the ring finger
[Dutch *ringvinger*] and is by very long tradition reserved
for a married woman's wedding ring and, sometimes, for
the engagement ring (promise ring) which precedes it and
which is moved to the right hand on marriage. In this
painting, the ring looks to me like a simple gold band and
in that case, it is almost certainly meant to be seen as a
wedding ring. So much for genre paintings of young girls
with fans. We are probably looking at a portrait of a married
or soon-to-be-married woman and this is surely a lead we
should follow up.

*

So who is the sitter? That question almost certainly has an
answer and at some point the answer was probably known
to the Rijksmuseum, which chose to ignore it – that is the
claim of a Dutch art historian, Dr Esther Schreuder. She did

some research into the provenance of this painting in connection with its use for a 2008 exhibition of paintings with black subjects, *Black is Beautiful*, and concluded that the painting came to the museum identified as a portrait of a named person. It was probably identified as a portrait of a Mrs Alting in which case the likely original and maybe artist's title for this painting is *Portrait of Mrs Alting*.

If it is true that this painting once had a title like that, I nonetheless have absolutely no explanation of why the Rijksmuseum chose to ignore it back in 1922 and didn't retrieve it in 2015. *Portrait of Mrs Alting* would be an appropriate gallery title and an expanded gallery description could then tell us who Mrs Alting was, to whom she was married (and maybe their respective ages at marriage) and whether (for example) this picture was painted as a marriage portrait - that might explain how she is dressed.

The answers to those questions probably exist in two archives not available on the Internet: the papers relating to the Andries van Wezel Bequest, held by the Rijksmuseum since 1922, and the Simon Maris family archives for which an outline catalogue can be found on the Internet; the contents themselves are in public custody in the Netherlands. Dutch registers of births, marriages and deaths should also be a source of further information and many are now available on the Internet.

The matter is not entirely straightforward because there is another version of this painting which on the Internet is identified as a portrait of a Mrs Allwood and a third version which identifies the sitter as Spanish (but which looks no different to the Mrs Allwood painting and may be the same one differently photographed). Both of these paintings, in a very different style to the Rijksmuseum painting, are signed Simon Maris but on the right rather than the left hand side. The Mrs Allwood painting was offered for sale by the Amsterdam auctioneers Glerum as recently as 2008. The auction catalogue said that it came from the De Visscher family in Zeist and that the family had got the painting from the artist in the 1920s. The painting was unsold and its current whereabouts unknown, though the auctioneers tell me they think it was sold privately through a gallery after the auction. It's possible that some kind of Chinese Whispers has been played out with the names - maybe Alting is the whispered version of Allwood or vice versa. But whatever the case, none of this is ancient history and somewhere it is documented.

It's a separate issue, but I merely note here that this painting does not look like the majority of Maris paintings you can find on the Internet and I simply don't know why. Likewise, it is rather puzzling that though Maris was living and working just round the corner from the Rijksmuseum on Keizersgracht, and well-known in Amsterdam at the time of the van Wezel bequest, it seems that he was not asked to date the painting (the range 1895 - 1922 is very wide for a modern work) or offer a title. And where was the sitter in 1922 and why wasn't the painting with her? It clutters up the simple morality tale I want to tell, but I have to say that lots of things in relation to this painting seem *not quite right*. The sitter does look very young to have a wedding ring, the painting does not look like Maris's regular work, the style could be that of a work painted many years before the dates (1895 - 1922) given to it.

*

But, leave aside those queries, why is my simple tale relevant to and important for political correctness?

If you turn a portrait of a particular person into a generic painting of a little negress or a young girl with a fan, then you deprive the original sitter of her identity. You also obscure the fact that the painting was worked out in the context of someone sitting for her portrait with someone whose business it was to make portraits. You obscure access to what the work is about. Crudely, there are differences between paintings where an artist has paid a model to sit and be painted as the *artist* chooses and paintings where someone has paid the artist to paint the sitter - and, usually, giving some attention to the way the *sitter* wants to be painted or the way the person paying wants them painted. Portrait painters normally work to commissions and Maris often did. Simon Maris was a "society" portrait painter who painted wealthy men and fashionable women. He was white and mostly they were white and quite often their portraits are identified by the name of the sitter. Some of course remain in private hands and the owners simply know who the portraits are portraits of. Some are clearly portraits but the sitter's name has been lost.

The letter of political correctness produces a bad result if it simply zaps out the word "Negress" or "Negro" and leaves us with someone (who might be anyone) holding a fan when that is not what the painting is all about. The spirit of correctness, in contrast, requires no more than this, that if a black woman sat for her portrait with Maris, then she should be accorded the same respect as would a white woman or a white man whose name would stay attached to the image. That is not a bureaucratic project in the adjustment of colonial terminology; it is about correctly understanding what is going on in the painting. If she was sitting for her own portrait, then this young black woman should have her name in its gallery title and gallery visitors thus allowed to appreciate that she is sitting for her own portrait at a time and place when what she is doing would have been quite unusual. Some explanation might be helpful, particularly if it could explain the conjunction of her youthful appearance and the presence of what looks like a wedding ring.

From open access Internet sources, there seems little room for doubt that this rather striking portrait was painted as a portrait of *someone* and the Rijksmuseum is probably in a position to tell us who she was and, perhaps also, who commissioned the painting. If so, it should now do so.

*

Postscript

I put the arguments developed above onto my personal Blog at the end of 2015 and sent copies to Dr Esther Schreuder (mentioned above) and to the Rijksmuseum. In January 2016, I got an email from Dr Jenny Reynaerts at the Rijksmuseum telling me that "we have started our research on the woman who was sitting for the painting and hope to adjust the neutral title soon". By early February 2016, the Rijksmuseum had withdrawn the title and description published in December 2015 and its website was showing the following revised title and description:

> *Young Woman with a Fan, Simon Maris, c. 1906*
> *oil on canvas, h 41 cm x w 29cm*
> *Simon Maris painted this woman on various occasions, holding a cigarette or a red fan. Perhaps she*

was a model, yet this painting could also be an actual portrait. For want of information, in the past it was variously titled as The Negress, Portrait of a Mulatto, East-Indian Type, The Little Negress. These terms are now considered derogatory. Until her name is known, the painting will bear a neutral title.

Z.

Now I know my ABC…

I can tell you that I began Blogging in 2010, probably some New Year's Resolution to remain Mentally Alert. Before then, and over several years, I had created an online home for my old academic work. The site was popular since the work was not abridged and there was no paywall. From the visitor information, it's likely that I am responsible for quite a few undergraduate essays. But the project was coming to an end. I had sixty essays on line, more than a quarter of a million words.

So, trying to stay alert for the next six years, I tapped out about half a million new words across the blogosphere. For anyone who has had to deal with the slowness of old-style academic publishing, instant and unhassled online publication provides a powerful hit. And whereas academic publications often fall dead-born from the press, unreadable or unread, the Internet allows you watch the numbers grow. My personal Blogs took me into six figures.

But not six figure readers. Six figure visitors. This is the downside. You have visitors who drop in on one thing you have written – say, about Marks and Spencer's men's socks (yes, I did) – but they don't go on to Follow you, to read more of what you are writing or to assess it. That is a main reason why, eventually, I began to think more kindly again about the printed word and the book form. You are more likely to get a reader than a visitor, and more likely to get someone who sticks with you at least part of the way and has a considered reaction at the end.

That said, a great deal of this book relies on open access Internet sources, located by Google and very often landing on Wikipedia pages. The previous chapter, *Young Girl with a Fan?* is entirely based on online open access sources. Elsewhere, it should be fairly obvious how to go about checking historical or other factual claims that I make.

I have kept the book short, a tour around my mind. I hope you got this far. And if you want men's socks, well, you will have to go to the Blogs since this book reworks only a fraction of all those Internet posts.

*

In converting Blogword to Bookword, I have been greatly assisted by Siân Rees, a determined editor who supplied me with hundreds of corrections, queries, suggestions and hints of exasperation. I acted on maybe half of her emailed notes in the margins and I hope she is more satisfied with this version of my work than the version with which we started in late 2015; I certainly am. She also suggested that I include something which showed my thinking on the topics which are now addressed in *War & Terror*.

Dr Esther Schreuder in Amsterdam responded to the first 2015 version of *Young Girl with a Fan?* mailed to her inbox and simply by treating it as a serious argument encouraged me to persist in developing my criticism of the work of a major public institution with which I had no previous involvement. But I should stress that responsibility for making that criticism is mine alone. At a later stage, Professor Ruth Bernard Yeazell at Yale University responded to another version, sent to her when I discovered that there was a new book out, *Picture Titles: How and Why Western Paintings Acquired Their Names* (Princeton UP 2015) of which she was the author. Her response helped me sharpen the use I make of the distinction between genre and portrait painting and her book would be essential reading for anyone who wanted to improve and expand on what there is in chapter Y. Suzanne Veldink at the Rijksmuseum corrected my Dutch and cleared up some confusion as to how the original story about the Museum's "Adjustment of Colonial Terminology" project came to appear in the press. For the substantive response of the Rijksmuseum, see the *Postscript* to chapter Y.

Ilva Kalnberza prepared the cover art work and Geoff Fisher did the typesetting. I am grateful to both of them and to Andy Howarth at the printing firm CPI who dealt effectively with numerous queries. Lark Parker-Rhodes kindly provided the author photograph.

Readers who have got this far and who have comments or enquiries are welcome to email me at:

trevor@trevorpateman.co.uk

About The Author

Trevor Pateman was born in England in 1947. After a state school education he studied at the universities of Oxford and London and spent a year at the École Pratique des Hautes Études in Paris as a pupil of Roland Barthes. His work on the foundations and implications of Chomskyan linguistics was published as *Language in Mind and Language in Society* (Oxford University Press 1987). He taught for twenty years at the University of Sussex and published academic studies on a wide range of topics in the humanities and social sciences. A large part of that work is now on open access at selectedworks.co.uk . He has active Blogs at trevorpatemanblog.com and readingthisbook.com

In case of any difficulty in ordering copies of this book online, please consult trevorpatemanblog.com for current suppliers